RAINBOW DARKNESS

an anthology of african american poetry

Poems and Essays from the
Diversity in African American Poetry Conference

Edited by
Keith Tuma

With Photographs by Lynda Koolish

Miami University Press
Oxford, Ohio

Other Titles from The Miami University Press

Poetry Series

General Editor: James Reiss

The Bridge of Sighs, Steve Orlen
People Live, They Have Lives, Hugh Seidman
This Perfect Life, Kate Knapp Johnson
The Dirt, Nance Van Winckel
Moon Go Away, I Don't Love You No More, Jim Simmerman
Selected Poems: 1965-1995, Hugh Seidman
Neither World, Ralph Angel
Now, Judith Baumel
Long Distance, Aleda Shirley
What Wind Will Do, Debra Bruce
Kisses, Steve Orlen
Brilliant Windows, Larry Kramer
After a Spell, Nance Van Winckel
Kingdom Come, Jim Simmerman
Dark Summer, Molly Bendall
The Disappearing Town, John Drury
Wind Somewhere, and Shade, Kate Knapp Johnson
The Printer's Error, Aaron Fogel
Gender Studies, Jeffrey Skinner
Ariadne's Island, Molly Bendall
Burning the Aspern Papers, John Drury
Beside Ourselves, Nance Van Winckel

Fiction Series

Edited by the Creative Writing faculty of Miami University

Mayor of the Roses, Marianne Villanueva

To the memory of Lorenzo Thomas

Library of Congress Cataloging-in-Publication Data

Diversity in African American Poetry Conference (2003 Miami University)
Rainbow darkness : an anthology of African American poetry poems and essays / from the Diversity in African American Poetry Conference ; edited by Keith Tuma.
p. cm. -- (The Miami University Press poetry series)
Poems presented at the conference held at Miami University in September 2003.
Includes bibliographical references.
1. American poetry--African American authors. 2. African Americans--Poetry. 3. American poetry--African American authors--History and criticism--Congresses. 4. African Americans--Intellectual life--Congresses. 5. African Americans in literature--Congresses. I. Tuma, Keith, 1957- II. Title. III. Series.
PS591.N4D575 2003
811'.6080896073--dc22 2005010184

The paper in this book meets the guidelines
for permanence and durability of the Committee
on Production Guidelines for Book Longevity
of the Council on Library Resources ♾

Printed in the U.S.A.

9 8 7 6 5 4 3 2 1

Contents

Preface

Rainbow Darkness is an anthology of poems and essays celebrating the Marjorie Cook Conference on Diversity in African American Poetry held at Miami University in September 2003. It hopes to extend the conversations that took place at the conference and to bring the poetry presented at it to another, larger audience. All of the contributors to the anthology attended the conference, and the poems included in it are among those read by poets who performed at the conference. Except for the plenary address by Lorenzo Thomas, which is slightly revised for inclusion here, the essays were solicited after the conference and written specifically for this book. I asked four among the many distinguished scholars and critics who presented papers at the conference to write about the situation of African American poetry in the new century, with some attention to the poems to be included here. My hope was that these four essayists, all of them accomplished poets as well as scholars, would take this admittedly vague assignment and define it for themselves. I wanted the anthology to be a collaborative project, and where possible I tried to stay out of the way and allowed the poets to pick the poems they wanted to have included — within the page counts enforced by budgets — and the essayists to say what they wanted to say.

The Marjorie Cook Conference on Diversity in African American Poetry was made possible by an endowment for poetry in the Department of English at Miami University. The endowment is named after its chief benefactor, the late Marjorie Cook, professor of English and later Associate Dean in the College of Arts and Science from 1967 until her death in 1985. For some years the Cook endowment sponsored visits to campus by nationally or internationally celebrated poets, but in early 2002 the Creative Writing faculty in Miami's Department of English decided that the purposes of the endowment would be better served by a bigger event, an event that might have a more lasting and broader impact, or so we hoped. We eventually determined that this event should be a national conference featuring readings by African American poets and scholarly papers about African American poetry. We wanted to present to our audience, which included the local population of Miami University and its surrounding communities as well as the poets and scholars participating in the conference, some of the poetry currently being written by African American poets, and to suggest the range of that poetry. Funds from the endowment supplemented by grants from the Ohio Arts Council and donations from various offices at Miami University, including the Department of English, Provost's Office, Office of Student Affairs, Center for American and World Cultures, Office of Liberal Education, and President James Garland, allowed us to invite the poets who are represented in this anthology and to host the event.

The funds at our disposal were not unlimited, of course, and we were not able to invite every African American poet or scholar of African American poetry worth inviting — far from it. We decided that we would try as best as we were able within our budget to invite poets who don't have a lot in common as poets, thereby hopefully encouraging conversations across some of the boundaries of practice, critical understanding, and affiliation that can divide poets. The most practical way to find poets who represented different poetic practices was to ask some of the poets and scholars then teaching poetry at Miami University — Annie Finch, Andrew Osborn, David Schloss, and your editor were the four who volunteered — to make lists of poets we wanted to invite to campus. Knowing that our interests overlapped in some ways but diverged in others, we each made our list of poets and then had a meeting to discuss our choices. Our discussions were informal. Nobody really wanted to go to the wall with his or her preferences or with the categories of poetic practice we discussed, which we recognized as fluid and provisional, terms allowing for conversation rather than labels finally defining any poet or tendency. We thought that we wanted to include poets whose practice extends the forms and practices of modernist and experimental poetry beside poets working in traditional forms. We wanted narrative poets and performance poets, oral traditions beside and mixed up with literary traditions. And so on — categories have a way of proliferating. If terms like "experimental" and "mainstream" have limited the readership of specific poetry or influenced this or that reader's engagement with it, we thought we might at least try to bring poets and critics and scholars together to initiate dialogues that looked past literary politics and acknowledged the impressive diversity of current poetic practice. After some compromising and discussing the proposed invitations with several other colleagues who were asked to join the committee — they are thanked below — we mailed our invitations. Nearly everybody invited decided to attend.

'Diversity' was one word we settled on for the name of our conference, though its other uses in discourses within and beyond academic institutions made for an ambiguity that was a little awkward. I remember wondering if as faculty at Miami University we were about to bring more African American poets to campus for one weekend — twenty names were listed on the conference poster — than had read at the university in the last five or maybe ten years. While we certainly hoped that the conference would help to promote awareness of the contributions of African Americans to American poetry, it was not the diversity of but rather the diversity in African American poetry that we meant to explore as a particular focus.

We might have chosen a phrase such as "infinite permutations" for the title of the conference, a phrase I take from a statement that Harryette Mullen made at another conference. We reproduced it as part of conference publicity:

> In our anxiety to embody or represent authentic black identity, we may impoverish our cultural heritage and simplify the complexity of our historical experience. As poets and as people of African descent, we are in danger of only performing blackness, rather than exploring the infinite permutations of our lived experience and creative imagination as black people.[1]

[1] Harryette Mullen, "What's African about African American Poetry?" *Fence* 4.1. Spring/Summer 2001. http://www.fencemag.com/v4n1/text/afric_amer.html.

Mullen's sense of the potential dangers of a rhetoric of authenticity is echoed by several essayists in this anthology, and I am tempted to wonder if the anthology represents a moment in the history of American poetry and African American poetry when some or even many African American poets are likely to disarticulate issues of poetic form from issues of cultural identity. Questions about how poetic practice relates to identity — whether we are talking about cultural, racial, ethnic, sexual, or national identity — now tend to be a part of an academic critical discourse in which most forms of essentialism are suspect, though I think it would be a mistake to imagine that the rejection of essentialist notions of identity for more nuanced, performative, or fluid models of identity equals the rejection of identitarianism per se.

Readers of this anthology will, I hope, be obliged to think about both commonalities and differences evident in the poetry and essays included herein. We wanted a conversation at the conference, and we were happy that discussions did not result in everybody more or less agreeing. And there was little consensus even as I tried to get the poets included here to agree upon a title for the anthology. Eight or nine titles were proposed, most of them using phrases from poems by canonical African American poets, but I could not get a single poet to sign on to a title proposed by another poet. In the end I was left to choose between my two favorites among those that had been proposed, "Bessie, bop, or Bach" from Langston Hughes's "Theme for English B" and "Rainbow Darkness" from Robert Hayden's "Theme and Variation." I opted at first for the phrase from the poem by Hughes because it speaks directly to the matter of several divergent streams as they inform African American poetic practice. As I have indicated, this was a key concept in imagining and organizing the conference. But I also admired the poem by Robert Hayden, in particular for its insistence on mutability and mystery, on a "changing permanence" and "an imminence / that turns to curiosa all I know." The optimism, the idea that light might be a "rainbow darkness / wherein God waylays us and empowers" — well, in the end, I couldn't resist. Let the phrase stand for the many possibilities for African American poetry still on the horizon.

Readers seeking to learn something about African American poetry in the new century will do well also to seek out the work of some of the other poets we considered inviting, including Miami University graduate Rita Dove, Erica Hunt, Jay Wright, Marilyn Nelson, Fred Moten, Amiri Baraka, Tracy K. Smith, Mark McMorris, Renee Gladman, Ed Roberson, Carl Phillips, Michael Harper, and many others whose work is mentioned in the essays included here and still others whose work can be found in *Hambone* and *Callaloo*, and a dozen other fine journals. We did invite Sonia Sanchez and Elizabeth Alexander, who planned to attend before events conspired against them. Because I think the point of this anthology should be to celebrate and document the conference, I did not ask Alexander and Sanchez for poems to include here. An ideal anthology would include their poems together with poems by the writers mentioned above and many others, but this book is what it is — a partial record of and print supplement to the conference.

I will conclude by thanking the people who helped make the conference and book possible. Thanks especially to Eric Goodman, Director of Creative Writing at Miami University, for his hard work in organizing the conference and festival, and to his assistant, Kelly Cowan, who worked many hours to see that everything went mostly without a glitch. Kelly Cowan's successor at Miami University Press, Jess Panzner, deserves thanks for her help with this book. Thanks also to Karen Shimizu, whose several roles in the department include work for the press, and to Kim Snow Logsdon for designing the book. Other colleagues in Miami's Department of English served on the conference committee and helped out with the conference. Thanks to all of them for their work and good humor: Helane Adams Androne, Stefanie Dunning, Cheryl Johnson, James Reiss, Rebecka Rutledge, and Michelle Taylor. Thanks especially to Cheryl Johnson for reading this preface, for her knowledge of the history of African American literature, and, most of all, for her wisdom and friendship. Last but not least, thanks to all of the scholars and poets who participated in or attended the conference, and especially to the poets and essayists whose work is presented in *Rainbow Darkness.*

Keith Tuma
May 2005
Oxford, Ohio

Evie Shockley

ALL OF THE ABOVE: MULTIPLE CHOICE AND AFRICAN AMERICAN POETRY

I voted but I'd rather not say which one I punched.
— *Harryette Mullen*

It doesn't seem like one should have to pass a test to be a poet. Certainly, the professions have their various entrance exams — the bar for lawyers, the boards for doctors, and the dissertation defense for professors — which are intended to keep the gates of each closed to all but the qualified, the trained, the privileged few. But poetry, which doesn't pay well, offer job security, or even make people famous (quick: name the U.S. Poet Laureate), ought logically to be open to anyone willing to spend time at it.

Yet African American poets have faced tests throughout the two and a half centuries that we have been writing poetry in this country. The example of Phillis Wheatley must come to mind for anyone familiar with the African American literary tradition. Wheatley, who was born in Africa and stolen into slavery around the age of nine, had written and published a book of poems before the U.S. was founded and before her own twentieth birthday. According to the front matter of the book, the publisher (who was located in England) was repeatedly warned that many members of the public would refuse to believe that an enslaved African — especially a young black girl — was capable of creating accomplished verse on the model of Alexander Pope's. To silence, or at least mute, such doubters, a group of "the most respectable Characters in Boston" — composed entirely of ruling class white men — was assembled to vouch for her as the true author of her poems. They attested: "She has been examined by some of the best Judges, and is thought qualified to write them."[1] We don't know precisely what form this examination took, but we can be sure that Wheatley's success was no mean feat.

[1] This "Attestation" is reproduced in *The Collected Works of Phillis Wheatley*, ed. John Shields, New York: Oxford UP, 1988, p. 7.

The kind of testing, however, that Wheatley underwent — meant to determine whether she, black and female, had the intellectual capacity to create her poems — is not the kind that troubles me today. In the 20th century, African American poets have more commonly been subjected to a different type of test: the poetics litmus test. Wheatley, I imagine, had to prove the broad range of her knowledge: of the English language, of Greek mythology, of traditional English poetic form, of the Christian Bible. By contrast, as applied to African American poets, the poetics litmus test measures, not ability or talent, but political allegiances and racial "authenticity." The litmus test knows no spectrum or middle ground; rather, it sorts things into two groups. The poetics litmus test — administered by critics, editors, audiences, and other poets — judges the poems we write and the poetics we espouse against a fairly rigid standard and declares us to be basically either one kind of poet or another. African American poets have typically faced one or both of two major litmus tests: one divides "authentically black" poets from "American" poets, the other divides "authentically black" poets from "avant-garde" poets.

The first of the two poetics litmus tests is used to separate poets whose fundamental loyalties are to the political struggles of blacks (in the U.S. and elsewhere) from poets who prioritize the crafting of technically accomplished, insightful, and linguistically beautiful lyric or narrative poetry. If this sounds reductive, it is. Nonetheless, African American poets whose poems do not primarily serve the perceived socio-political needs of black people have typically failed to earn the designation "authentically black." The meaning of this designation has changed over time in response to changes in American society and the political landscape, as well as new movements in other artistic fields (such as music, visual art, and dance). For instance, during the New Negro Renaissance era, black critics and audiences expected African American poets to write about racial subjects, or to racially mark so-called universal themes, in ways that would demonstrate to white readers how "human" (vs. animal), how "modern" (vs. primitive), and how "normal" (vs. different from whites) black folks are. The "middle-class values" of white audiences (who purchased the vast majority of black authors' books) greatly influenced the image of blackness that was deemed desirable. Langston Hughes, among others, bucked this trend and began to portray the "black masses" in his poems, emphasizing their cultural difference from whites *as well as* their humanity, and thus laying the groundwork for a different definition of "authentic blackness" that would really come into its own in the 1960s during the Black Arts Movement (BAM). Since the heyday of BAM and the "black aesthetic" (its Afrocentric philosophy of art), the litmus test has reserved the "authentically black" designation for poets whose work not only depicts blacks as *essentially* different from whites, but also addresses itself directly to black audiences, offering political analysis and social commentary in language accessible to the less-educated majority of the black community.

I don't mean to give the impression that this litmus test originated with black poets, critics, and readers. No, the dominant sector of American poetry — what we frequently and imprecisely refer to as the "mainstream" — also administers this litmus test to African American poets. Indeed, the "authentically black" designation initially developed, in large part, as a response to the exclusion of African American writers from the white literary establishment, specifically, and to American racism, generally. To receive the appellation "American" poet (or at least to be eligible for it), an African American poet has had to avoid writing in styles or about subjects that are recognizably "black" in favor of "universal" themes and conventional aesthetics. *Or* she could slip in the back door by appearing willing to narrate "the black experience" for white consumption in ways that do not fundamentally deconstruct white (liberal) understandings of race or directly advocate revolutionary social change. (In other words, a certain amount of "blackness" is acceptable within the American poetry tradition, so long as it confirms what white people know about us poor, angry, long-suffering, passionate, entertaining black folks.) While a few African American poets have acquired the "American" poet designation in each period of the 20th century, the litmus test has operated most often to exclude African

American poets from the "mainstream" tradition or banish them to the tradition's outskirts. It can be a lose-lose situation for some African American poets. The two poetic camps define themselves to some degree against one another, particularly insofar as political engagement is the touchstone of the former, while the latter insists that politics are antithetical to aesthetics and should be subordinated to the mastery of craft. African American poets interested in transgressing the boundary between these two approaches, when faced with the poetics litmus test, have had to accept the terms of one of them, to refuse those terms and have a label imposed upon them, or, perhaps worst of all, to face rejection by both camps.

The second litmus test divides the "authentically black" poets from the "avant-garde" poets. While the "avant-garde" designation is available to poets who understand poetry and politics to be related rather than antithetical (especially during the era of L=A=N=G=U=A=G=E poetry), the contours of that relationship differ ultimately from the politics/poetry connection affirmed by the standards for "authentic blackness." The "avant-garde" poet locates the proper challenge to the political status quo in formal experiments designed to disrupt the powerful hegemony of the structures of genre and of language itself. Of course, formal innovation has frequently (though not always) constituted a notable element of "authentically black" poetry, insofar as it has objected to the Eurocentric bias perceived to be inherent in traditional prosody and received forms. The desire to de-center Anglo-American aesthetics and ideologies has led to the development of new forms rooted in African American (or African) culture, such as the blues stanzas originated and popularized by Hughes and Sterling Brown, and of unorthodox spellings and typography intended to reflect nonstandard black speech patterns, as evident in many poems by Amiri Baraka and Sonia Sanchez, for example. Given that this politicized understanding of aesthetics has long been a feature of "authentically black" poetry, it's ironic that African American poets have consistently had to face this second litmus test — all the more so because, like black poetry, avant-garde poetry has never been allowed squarely under the banner of American poetry. (The avant-garde's intellectualism and its roots in non-Anglophone literary movements, like surrealism, have disqualified it from full inclusion in the American poetic "mainstream.") But neither their shared state of exclusion nor their common oppositional stance vis-à-vis the dominant modes of American poetry has been able to overcome the avant-garde allergy to narrative deployment of the lyric "I" or the black aesthetic commitment to identity politics. Because these two politicized poetics diverge so radically — black aesthetics toward accessibility and the incorporation of black popular culture, and avant-garde aesthetics toward difficulty and defamiliarization — the divide between them has arguably been even deeper than that between "authentically black" and "American" poetics.

So why do these poetics litmus tests matter? What is at stake for African American poets in the designations they receive or don't receive? The cynical answer is "career"; the more generous reply is "community." By either name, I want to suggest that the shape of a poet's writing life, creatively and publicly, and the fate of her poetry in the long-term are directly related to (sometimes largely determined by) the results of her poetics litmus test(s). As I noted above, the administrators of these tests are other poets, critics (including literary scholars), editors, and audiences — admittedly overlapping groups — all of whom generally act, within their specific roles, in accordance with the test results. That is, decisions about who to read, who to review, who to teach, who to publish, who to invite to give readings, and who to go hear read are frequently made with reference to the "black," "American," and "avant-garde" designations and the different assumptions that attach to each. Though the writing of poetry is at core a fairly solitary process involving the poet and her pen or keyboard, a poet who seeks to grow in her craft and reach an audience outside of her own circle of intimates will generally find the value of a poetic community to be considerable — Emily Dickinson (and, perhaps, Jay Wright) notwithstanding. The communities come complete, as it were, with a circle of contemporaries, a constellation of acceptable influences, a demarcated group of publishing outlets, and a target audience; thus their limitations are also their advantages. Poetic communities help make a poet's work visible to critics and audiences; they also facilitate the exchange of ideas that push poets to reach deeper or venture out into unfamiliar territory. Journals and presses are often established to provide a publishing outlet for the members of a poetic community.[2] Critics familiar with the work coming out of a particular community over time are likely to be more willing and better able to engage that poetry and to interpret and contextualize it for potential audiences. More and more, the poets who are remembered — those whose work is published and reviewed throughout their career and/or eventually canonized and studied by scholars — tend to be those who have had (or posthumously gain) the support of a strong poetic community.

Not only does the canon reflect and respond to these factors. Most poets, I believe, are aware of these considerations and consciously make choices based on the predictable — though not inevitable — consequences. These pressures can influence a poet's writing in ways that we may or may not applaud. I can think of numerous examples. Compare Hughes with William Stanley Braithwaite, a poet and critic who published two books of poetry during the early 1900s. As he explains in his autobiography, Braithwaite wanted his poetry to be appreciated (by white American critics and audiences) without regard to his race; therefore, he refused to include any racial markers in his traditionally rhymed and metered poems. Perhaps his choice was partially (even understandably) influenced by the schizophrenic fate of his poetic predecessor Paul Laurence Dunbar, who felt he had to put his formal, standard English verse aside to produce the entertaining "Negro dialect poems" that white audiences loved.[3] By contrast, Hughes made Harlem his ur-setting and the blues both his subject and his form — a decision that was not universally popular with his contemporary

---

[2] Famously, *Poetry* magazine was founded in 1912 by Harriet Monroe as a vehicle for the new modernist poets; a more contemporary example is giovanni singleton's *nocturnes (re)view,* which is devoted to, in her words, "creative voices... throughout the African Diaspora and other contested spaces" and "the exploration of spirit through innovative (i.e. experimental/avant-garde) critical and creative literary art." (See singleton's introduction to the 2001 premier issue.)

[3] James Weldon Johnson references Dunbar's dilemma in the original preface to *The Book of American Negro Poetry*, ed. Johnson, 2nd ed., reprint, San Diego: Harcourt, 1969 (pp. 35-36), as well as in the biographical statement on Dunbar (pp. 50-51).

African American audiences, as evidenced by the discussion in his essay "The Negro Artist and the Racial Mountain," even though it led to some of his most valued contributions to the tradition. But ultimately Hughes's poems identified him as a "black poet," to the eventual approval of African American critics and popular audiences — and to the relief of white ones, who (by ignoring certain aspects of his later work, like its communist politics or its high-cultural allusions) could safely compartmentalize him as an "authentic" folk artist. Braithwaite, on the other hand, has been forgotten with regard to the American tradition to which he aspired and is severely marginalized within the African American poetic canon, where he is known almost entirely for his work as a critic. We could similarly compare the divergent responses of Robert Hayden and Gwendolyn Brooks to the trumpet blast of BAM in the 1960s — when Hayden refused to conform his poetics to black aesthetic mandates while Brooks wholeheartedly embraced them — and look at the critical responses then and since. Or in the contemporary moment, we could consider what Harryette Mullen has said about the ways her writing has shifted as she responds to the competing expectations of her black and non-black audiences as well as her own complex aesthetic concerns.[4] These brief examples, I hope, will provide some sense of the scope of this issue. The repercussions of the poetics litmus test results are incredibly wide-ranging, with immediate and long-run significance for the poets themselves and for the tradition of African American poetry.

* * *

Enter the Marjorie Cook Diversity in African American Poetry Conference — not alone or even out front, but as one of a growing number of institutions (such as Cave Canem)[5] and ad hoc gatherings (in person and in print) designed to foster a poetic community that

[4] See Mullen's "Imagining the Unimagined Reader" (pp. 403-05) and Elisabeth A. Frost's "'Sleeping With the Dictionary': Harryette Mullen's 'Recyclopedia'" (especially p. 415), both in *American Women Poets in the 21st Century: Where Lyric Meets Language*, ed. Claudia Rankine and Juliana Spahr, Middletown: Wesleyan UP, 2002.

[5] Cave Canem ("Beware the Dog" in Latin) is the workshop/retreat for African American poets founded in 1996 by Toi Derricotte and Cornelius Eady.

does not administer a poetics litmus test, but is based instead on a *different* kind of test: multiple choice.

Are you:

a) a black poet (that is, deeply influenced by the black aesthetic)?
b) an American poet (that is, invested in perfecting conventional lyric poems written in traditional forms or free verse)?
c) an avant-garde poet (that is, committed to disrupting discourse, exploring the space of the page, and challenging the boundaries of the genre)?
d) a & b?
e) a & c?
f) b & c?
g) all of the above?

This anthology attests to the assembly at Miami University of Ohio in September 2003 of a group of poets and literary scholars interested in the exchange of words, poems, and ideas across the boundaries between poetic camps. It attests to the fact there is now (again? more than ever?) a critical mass of African American poets who refuse to recognize a poetic form or experimental approach as "white," if "white" means "off-limits to black poets" — regardless of whether the prohibition is motivated by white racism or black self-defense. These poets insist on their right to take up specifically racial subjects or themes that have no direct relation to race, to include or not include easily identifiable "blackness" in their poems, as they see fit. They aren't glossing black cultural references — thanks to some hard-won struggles with the academy and the publishing industry, readers can go look up and read up on who's who and what's what in black history and black life, just like we can figure out who Botticelli is when he shows up in a poem. These poets communicate articulately in black vernacular and they be droppin them big dictionary words, too. They aren't apologizing for their degrees nor are they disdainful of the solid education many obtain outside of classrooms.

And what does this anthology yield, as a result? Diversity, in a more meaningful sense than I have come to expect based on my last ten years of experience in the academy. There could have been more diversity at this conference: Tracie Morris had to hold it down for spoken word all on her own; there's a brand of down home, Southern, rural black poetry that Crystal Williams was representing virtually solo; and Sonia Sanchez, who was blocked from attending by Hurricane Isabel, would have been the only emissary from the core of the Black Arts Movement. To be fair, these choices may have reflected the organizers' perception that these styles of poetry typically receive the bulk of attention given to the African American tradition (which is true of black popular audiences, but less true within the largely white halls of academe). Be that as it may, there was a broad spectrum of themes, subjects, formal strategies, and stylistics offered by poets of various geographical regions, class origins, genders, sexualities, and political persuasions. The anthology reflects this diversity — not only among the poets, but within many of the poets' individual selections.

Look in these pages for the formalist verse of James Richardson, who transforms a vodoun loa into a villanelle and reinvigorates the tired concept of multiculturalism with a (Japanese) haiku sequence in which the Greek muses are interpreted through contemporary African American experience: "Calliope, muse of epic poetry" smiles as "Rappers slice airwaves" like "afroed Beowulves." Richardson revels in the productive tensions of such juxtapositions, as does Anthony Walton in his poem "Dissidence," in which he weds the "dissonance-driven explorations" of Thelonious Monk to the neat, exquisite couplets of his poem. "[Y]ou have to disagree with everything except the piano," Walton says of/to Monk, a line that speaks like a brief allegorical ars poetica for the body of work this anthology collects. Wanda Coleman serves up a similar friction in a poem entitled "Metaphysically Niggerish," which imagines in vivid, erudite language the recovery of "buried" African history and the rise of African rule over the West. She slaps a mortarboard on the n-word and keeps stepping.

These poems link different kinds of "blackness" and critiques of racism to a variety of other socio-political concerns. Coleman, for example, injects grief with rage in "Notes on a Departure." The mother wails not only her individual pain, but a litany of psychic and physical injuries suffered by gay men in our homophobic society. Her speaker asks: "what has made / and kept us the freak children of the universe? // what evil says our deaths are deserved?" These questions might apply to heterosexual blacks just as easily as to homosexual men, as the poem indicates when it says "to know blackness is to know bereavement." Tracie Morris explodes the black vernacular in her "Apology to Pangea" for the environmental havoc wreaked by humans with our bombs and other nasty habits: "Can I say sorry for dem sweep yo feet, Mam?" On the same wavelength is Nathaniel Mackey's "Song of the Andoumboulou: 62," part of his ongoing series, inspired by Dogon cosmology, about the troubled tribe of rough-draft humans that seem suspiciously like us. He obliquely critiques the current war against Iraq, locating us (blacks? other disempowered Americans?) in a place of relative safety, but also perhaps complicity: "Planes flew... Bombs fell... / Operation Boast. Operation Lie. / Thug regime scrimmaging thug / regime, we were in the middle." "[W]e" aren't the target, but "we" are, as Americans, in the thick of things — and thus risk becoming what is euphemistically called collateral damage. Kim Hunter's "no like place" addresses the intersection of race and class, deflating an old African American sacred cow with wicked wordplay. In black Detroit, three horses becomes two ("one is at the pawn shop") becomes one, because it turns out that the third "one was a rat on stilts / trying to get a job / with the mounted police / on belle isle / it's all about uplift."

In this collection, traditional lyric and narrative poems sit comfortably beside prose poems, disjunctive poly-vocal poems, and poems that stretch, bend, and shatter language in an attempt to communicate, fleetingly, something outside the hegemonic ideological box. Identifiably "black" poems commune with poems in which race is beside the point. Natasha Trethewey's bitter lullaby for "Bellocq's Ophelia" rubs elbows with Tyrone Williams' disembodied but pointed communiqués on our consumer-driven society ("Plan B — Walk, Listen"). Honorée Jeffers' spiritual blues, calling on Mary in the name of thwarted motherhood, hugs Mendi Lewis Obadike's revision of the "Protest Poem," which, instead of directing rage at white America, invokes the "sweetness" and "cool... shade" that the oppressed will need to survive the "pressing," "aching," and "burn[ing]" we face. Terrance Hayes' "Nothing," in which blackness is simply a given, coexists peacefully with Reginald Shepherd's "Refrain," in which race is a footnote. C. S. Giscombe, in his cerebral yet conversational prose poem "Light, Bright, Etc.," calls for an "end of [the] hoop-la" about skin color, which he sees as ultimately a cover for more fundamental problems. "Skin stands in," he says; "I'm as interested as I should be." And so on: the visionary humor of Tim Seibles' dramatic monologues, the self-described "mythic improvisation" of Jeffrey Allen's sparsely punctuated stanzas, and, of course, the take-no-prisoners (take-no-sides) truth-telling of Lorenzo Thomas — all amicably at home with one another in one volume.

Or maybe these various and sundry poetics, topics, and perspectives don't mesh as easily and seamlessly as all that, after all. Maybe, among the many wonderful poems and poets collected here, there are some contradictions, some jarring discontinuities; maybe there is some chafing and some awkwardness. Maybe it's about time these discordancies were sounded. Be-bop struck some ears roughly, too, at first.

All of the above. Do we want to retain the poetics litmus tests, as we move into the 21st century with African American poetry? Harryette Mullen suggests something quite telling about the kind of choices the litmus tests present, in her poem "Bumper to Bumper." She riffs off the pervasive bumper sticker slogan: *I'd rather be...golfing*. Or *fishing*. Or, in her example, "at the beach." We are supposed to understand these inviting pastimes and locations as preferred alternatives to driving, as Mullen makes clear: "I'm stuck in traffic when I'd rather be surfing." The various alternatives invoked by these bumper stickers always seem to require a good bit of money or, at least, of leisure. Mullen draws our attention to this elitist, consumerist discourse by creating similar "slogans" that expose how futile such expressed preferences are for the legions of people who can't afford to execute them. Many people who might indeed "rather be at the beach" will rarely, if ever, have the time and money to go. In a society that constructs freedom as the ability to purchase anything you choose, such alternatives are essentially Hobson's choices, *non-choices,* for the nation's poor (not to mention poor people globally), as her concluding lines illustrate: "I'd rather work than starve. I'd rather drink unfiltered tap water and sleep on a lumpy futon than live anywhere else in this godforsaken world." With choices like these, who needs ultimatums?

The poetics litmus tests — *black poet or American poet? black poet or avant-garde poet?* — appear to offer real choices. But, in fact, many African American poets, needing to find a nurturing, reliable community in which to work, have felt pressure to modify their identities and mold their poetics to fit the expectations that audiences and critics have for black writers. Those who refuse have risked being outcast by the racial community, with no guarantee that largely white communities — traditional or avant-garde — would take them in. Aesthetic choices made under such conditions aren't really choices at all.

I celebrate the spirit that generated a conference on Diversity in African American Poetry. I'm thrilled that these poems (and poets and critics) are talking to one another — even to disagree — under the auspices of one conference and within the covers of a single book, rather than talking at one another from different publications and different events. We who gathered at this conference, and you who read this anthology, have a richer, fuller sense of the vast possibilities of African American poetry, precisely because so many different voices were brought together. Potential cacophony, potential choir.

Aldon Nielsen

"AIN'T GONNA LET NOBODY TURN ME AROUND"

so we are stuck with our history
with lips pursed over jello
and nervous young cops
guns un-holstered at night
after the school burns down
— Kim Hunter

Mickey I think of you, I think you
into my body,
jelly tissue beginnings soft parts
in the loam of a dam between Philadelphia and Meridian
— Armand Schwerner

"Oxford," for me, was an ominous sound, the sound of murder and racism. First heard in the odd intonations of television news men, those two syllables weighed heavily on my youth. Bob Dylan wrote a song about it. I didn't know who Bob Dylan was, but my older sister had the record. "Oxford town, Oxford town," the song began, over an unusual guitar pattern. "Better get away from Oxford town," the song advised. For me, this Oxford, forever joined with a murder in Mississippi, *was* Oxford. It was only later I learned of its namesake in England; later still that I began to learn of still other Oxfords. We all had a lot to learn in the sixties, which is why you can see such pained looks on our faces, we "boomers," as we contend with those among our countrymen still refusing to learn the lessons of America's own soul. Didn't learn from Lincoln's second inaugural address; didn't learn from Oxford; we still stand in a place where the color of a voter's skin may determine the way the die is cast, or if the vote is counted at all. Each town is twinned in America's racial cosmology. Philadelphia, we learned in school, is the city of brotherly love. Philadelphia, Mississippi, we learned from our news announcers, a town nearly drowned in the bloody history of Klan violence, was the place Ronald Reagan chose to take his stand, aiding and abetting those who would seek refuge in "states rights" from the demands of democracy, those who would appeal to abstractions of federation to deny any appeal from the majority of their fellow citizens, their darker brothers. *Meridian* is the second novel by Alice Walker. A meridian demarcates, and along that line lies the dam, next-to-last resting place of James Chaney, Andrew Goodman, and Mickey Schwerner. Follow a line of demarcation out from Peabody Hall at Miami University and you arrive at a little piece of Mississippi in Ohio, stone cast on a rise in the earth, calling to mind the earthwork tomb from which Chaney, Goodman and Schwerner rose. It's a very different Cheney on our minds these days, but in 1964, supporters of the Mississippi Freedom Democratic Party held vigil outside the Democratic convention, holding up pictures of Chaney, Schwerner and Goodman, who had met their deaths in Mississippi earlier that same Summer, acting in a cause openly opposed by George H.W. Bush and Dick Cheney and now by a newer, yet more glib generation.

On the stone works across from Peabody Hall, lines inscribed in stanzaic patterns recount the events of 1964, events that irrevocably linked Oxford, Mississippi with Oxford, Ohio. This I had never known. I knew already that an earlier troupe of activists attempting to integrate interstate bus systems in the Jim Crow south had sought solace in the hilly refuge of Black Mountain College, which has its own mythic place in the history of American poetry. It took a poetry conference for me to learn that prior to their travel to Mississippi Freedom Summer and its attendant dangers, many of the young activists had gathered at Oxford's Western College for Women. The first group left Ohio for the segregated south on June 20th, 1964. On June 21st, Chaney, Goodman and Schwerner, names forever conjoined in this awful announcement, were reported missing in Mississippi. It was another six weeks before their corpses were unearthed. The Democratic Party was to finesse the demands of the Mississippi Freedom Democrats that year. Four years later, Richard Nixon and the Republicans would cement their "Southern Strategy," a long march that has reproduced a twin of the old "solid south" for our time. In 1967, just three years after the murder of the trio of civil rights workers, LeRoi Jones (Amiri Baraka) was on trial for charges trumped up in the swirl of the Newark uprisings. It was in the course of that proceeding that Baraka heard the trial judge read Baraka's own poetry from the bench as evidence against him. Among the poets gathering to defend Baraka against this outrage was Armand Schwerner, whose poem "speech for LeRoi," memorializes Schwerner's cousin Mickey and the moment of martyrdom. "Belief in the poem / requires a major transplant every morning," Schwerner wrote, and read at the rally calling for Baraka's release. At the 2004 Democratic Convention, African American activists spoke from the podium, not just from the aisles, recalling the blood-soaked legacy of the right to vote, calling to mind the three young men in Mississippi, the four young girls of Condoleezza Rice's Birmingham, the many thousands gone.

And so it was a calling to come among believers that went out from Miami University. Like so many others, I took a moment to register the fact that it was Miami University in Ohio that was organizing a conference on black American poetries, and to reassure myself that this Oxford was not the one Bob Dylan sang of, that Tom Paxton sang of, that the Freedom Singers called out. Still, it seemed a white place to one who had never been there, 'till, that is, I was there, standing in front of that memorial, a joint project of the Oxford NAACP, the Friends of the Mississippi Summer Project and Miami University. If belief in the poem, when we are seemingly stuck with our history, requires a transplant every morning, this might prove a good place to greet the sunrise. Though a hurricane intervened.

The printed program returned to its status as work-in-progress as the good people of Miami U, their ears glued to cell phones, took call after call from anxious poets and critics finding themselves in the hurricane's path. As thousands of trees fell along the Virginia coast, as Sonia Sanchez sat in her darkened house wondering at the depth of the water, those who could, came. Most could, and in their coming paid small tribute to those who came before. The conference T-shirt, with its optimistic list of participants, soon became a sign of just what a miracle could be made out of the "could have been." The weather in Oxford itself was a wonder, the eye of a poetic storm raging out of our past across our mutual landscape. If you couldn't miss the missing, it was only because there was so much to attend to on the ground. Those of us who have been in the storm a long time, which is to say all poets, attend to the language with an ear cocked for connotations. Those of us with listening posts in early twenty-first century America's academic culture have learned a particular suspicion of the word "diversity," a word around which entire industries of workshops and human resources training have been spawned, a word that all too conveniently lets many feel that we have come a good deal farther than we have in fact come. So the appearance of the word "diversity" in the subtitle of the Miami University conference was unsettling weather of its own. But those same T-shirts, both before and after the deluge, were reassurance, with their listing of poets running the gamut from the established church to the most raucous store-front. For once, diversity was no mere diversion, was rather what we have promised ourselves all along: *e pluribus unum.*

This was in evidence every day of the gathering. One night jolted students convened in the large auditorium from the attentive quiet (punctuated by polite epiphanies) with which they have learned to attend to things so serious as verse, when Wanda Coleman slammed her book down onto the heavily amplified podium. It was jump up time, and even those who thought they knew what stand up and performance and spoken word meant in American poetry found themselves confronted by a poet not willing to accept assignment readily to any of those categories. Coleman had been shifted on the program, due to the hurricane's having finally stopped Sonia Sanchez in her tracks, and found herself on a program with Nathaniel Mackey and Harryette Mullen. Mackey's way is quieter in person yet perhaps louder on the page. Mullen, accompanied by her favorite sleeping companion, the dictionary, turned a few new pages not only for students but for even the most vocable of vocabulary wielders in the room.

The hurricane, it happens, had made that evening a California affair, giving the conference the chance to register in one evening's offerings the remarkable range of black verse on the Pacific rim. Earlier that same day the conference had heard Lorenzo Thomas's plenary address. Thomas, friend to Mullen from her Texas days, stood as a link back to the Umbra group and to the very cusp of the Black Arts era, and his talk swept from the Slim Greer poems of Sterling Brown to the commercial appearances of Ziggy Marley. Diversity danced from the fringe to the scrum.

There were moments when one was instantly transported back to those halcyon days when students actually stalked their campuses with little books of poetry stuffed into the hip pockets of their blue jeans, or at least I was so transported when I heard two participants on one days' panel suddenly disputing the efficacy of Swahili terminology; I was there when that bone was picked over forty years before, when "rapping" referred to those endless debates through the night we all had in little clumps of vociferous intellect, and here I was again. You come too. This was important, that the critical debates of the weekend fostered every bit as much diversity as did the major series of readings. On one panel we witnessed the newer generation of poet/critics, as Evie Shockley and Mendi Lewis Obadike presented their work on a panel titled, appropriately enough for this hurricane-ravaged conference, "Missing Pieces." Tyrone Williams on a panel that same day addressed that "curious thing," authenticity (yes, we're still having that debate as well), analyzing the critical reception of Ed Roberson's work. In his own reading, shifted to fill the slot formerly held by Wanda Coleman when she had been shifted to fill the spot formerly held by Sonia Sanchez, Williams presented work of a sort to demand that we understand "authentic" as the modifier that it is, not as some measurable serum to be injected into a poem. The critical talks, rampaging as they did across the broadest plains of African American literary history, and ranging across a critical landscape that unfolded from the nearly inaudible formalisms of Anthony Walton to the performative critique of Tracie Morris, who was sitting in a chair as she delivered her paper despite her seeming to be flying through the air, were never seen as an add-on to the readings, simply as providing a forum for attendees who needed to give a paper in order to get departmental support for their travel. What was in full effect here, though it was not an announced subject of the conference, was the insistent return of the poet-critic to the stage, especially important when one considers the lack of attention the American academy has given to the category of the poet-critic in African American letters. (What, Houston Baker writes poetry? You're kidding, right? There were black critics before Henry Louis Gates? African American thinkers think about, gasp, the philosophy of poetics?) While so many academics are entertaining themselves with the eighty-fifth book from a university press that explains how the now-quarter-of-a-century old Hip Hop is a transgressive, cutting edge counter-hegemonic cultural production, black critics are, as Anna Everett has been telling us for years, in the house.

There were still stars in the firmament even after the storm broke the predicted constellations, but there were new patterns to be discerned at Oxford, new unheard-of blues, new changes in the "changing same." In Lorenzo Thomas's plenary address, he spoke to us of two directions traceable in contemporary African American poetry, and it is striking how those two directions in some significant ways track the two worn and wearing modes of critical reception historically afforded black verse in Thomas's schema. For him, these two critical responses have formed a vexatious backdrop to the evolving modes of black poetic invention. For it would seem that even while the oral basis of African American poetry has lead, if anything, to black verse as a "locus of stylistic and formal innovation," the critical emphasis upon orality has tended to sharply narrow the range of poetries celebrated and rewarded with a curricular niche. Meanwhile, poets who "chose to work in traditional or *current* poetic styles" [and doesn't that pretty much cover the territory?], according to Thomas, are often derided as "derivative, imitative, or — if they do it very well — uppity." Now, you're not likely to find "uppity" listed among the terms of criticism in any introductory text on poetics currently in use in the American academy, but neither are you likely to locate there poetry that truly tests the critical expectations of what black poetry is supposed to be. Four decades after Amiri Baraka wrote "How You Sound," it remains curious what does and does not sound black to American readers of poetry.

Which brings us to a curious pass in the first decade of our new century. Thomas remarks "a tension" between the highly valorized oral tradition "and those who are interested in exploiting their inheritance of the English-language literary tradition." Let the proper weight fall on those words "their inheritance." Thomas says that this is what comes of growing up in America, and the situation he describes is an odd sort of double-unconsciousness. In the academy, the world of African American poetry has been fairly well divided up among the mainstream, workshop style, personal narrative lyric mode that has been awarded with Pulitzer prizes, university press publication and MFA programs, and the Spoken Word mode, which has developed its own realm of slams, open mic nights, festivals, and now off-Broadway productions. One of the oddities of this situation is that while the mainstream lyric mode is the most prized among the inhabitants of creative writing programs (though none of those inhabitants is likely fully to foreswear the rhetorical possibilities of Spoken Word style performance), the world of rap and Hip Hop has come for many academic critics to stand as a synecdoche for the whole of black poetry. Too often overlooked in this division of spoils are the many ways in which the legacy of the Black Arts Movement, itself a child of the era of Chaney, Schwerner and Goodman, have been exploding in new formations all around us.

This problem, too, is two-fold. On the one hand, beginning in the late 1970s, there was a strong reaction against certain felt experiences of the Black Arts among younger poets working in the more mainstream modes. Several essays appeared quite rightly taking the Black Arts Movement to task for essentialist moments, self-defeating bouts of chauvinism and what was now seen as a nationalist dead-end. Little-noted at the time, at least in the academy, was the fact that many of the most powerful critiques of these failings were leveled by Black

Arts poets themselves, Amiri Baraka being perhaps the most visible example. The criticisms soon, however, jelled into a cliché every bit as destructive as that which was being criticized, and it has taken all the intervening years for critics and literary historians to make a proper beginning towards recovering the full diversity of the Black Arts. We are only now, for example, starting to see serious critical attention to the likes of Carolyn Rogers as a new generation of scholars and readers undertake the revising of the received wisdom regarding the Black Arts. At the same time, the cultural legacy of the Black Arts Movement was all too easily ceded to those who stepped forward to inhabit the tone and posture of the nationalist poets but who seemingly had little patience for the serious aesthetic heavy lifting that had been on the agenda in the 1960s. If the search for a Black Aesthetic had gotten stranded somewhere out on the essentialist deserts, the truly radical poetics of much of the work of that era was overlooked all together. Contemporary poets of the Spoken Word school are often heard advancing the same pleas for a populist aesthetic that were heard in the late 60s, and yet, while many poets today will adopt the tone and performance style of Baraka, very few will write poems that look anything like the radical forms he has been exploring for the past half century.

But, like the jazz that served as Baraka's inspiration, the more radical aesthetic impulse has never gone away. The bridge was most visible at the conference in the persons of poets like Nathaniel Mackey, Harryette Mullen and C. S. Giscombe. In "Negromania, Negrophilia, Negrophobia," Giscombe writes "any song would straighten you. The sum of the songs is you singing an *old* cover of the divine portent, you come to that." This is Al Young's "song turning back on itself," Baraka's "dance that punishes speech." This is the open field running of black projections in verse. Frost wrote, "you come too," but he didn't seem to have black readers in mind in his invitation. "Get to that," we used to say in the 60s. Giscombe's inviting, imprecating second person is portentous in the best sense of the old school; its opening out at the end, like the minister who invites the newly chosen to come down to the front of the church, sketches the radical democracy on all sides advocated equally by Melville and Baraka. Similar moments were everywhere in evidence in Oxford as the storm passed over us. There in the recent explorations of Tracie Morris, the new found sounds (though he's been writing them for years) of Tyrone Williams (and you'd *better* call, Tyrone), the addled dictionaries of Harryette Mullen, the irritable mystics of Mackey's stuttering songs, even in the sounds of the hurricane preventing poets from getting there. And just where is it you have come to?

Take a look, just to choose two from among the plethora of possibles (what, you want to contend with Jeff Allen? You want me to drop some Kim Hunter on you?), just take a look at two good friends on the program: Evie Shockley and Mendi Lewis Obadike. In two songs of the South, these two poets sing, as Obadike says of someone in her poem, "some tough else." I can imagine what might be said of this line in some workshops, and could probably do a fair imitation of the fair and unfair practicing their white arts against this poem. It's all there in the title, "Tradition/Abstraction." Black poems are supposed to be in the tradition, and this one is. Black poems are supposed to memorialize Tupac and Biggie, the way we used to elegize Trane, and this poem does. But, despite the evidence of a thousand years of African art traditions, Americans get weird in the presence of black abstraction. And here we have a poem "after Gilberto Gil," about a girl visiting Atlanta. "This was when we still protested Freaknik." (As it happens, one year's meeting of the College Language Association overlapped Freaknik in Atlanta — you should have seen the faces of the students when they got on the hotel elevators, looked up and saw professors staring them in the face.) There's a delicious tension between the memories of Tupac and Biggie and the thought of what it was about Freaknik that would lead to protests (at least, protest from black folk). But what I like best about this poem, the "some tough else" that I love, is the walking, singing and thinking. Thinking while black, still a crime in most of America.

And then look at Evie Shockley's "cause i'm from dixie too." It starts out, "i am southern hear me roar," and if you don't get that allusion you are hereby sentenced to 48 hours of continuous reruns of the *Helen Reddy Show*. Two score and some years ago, Amiri Baraka wrote a short story in which he promised the crackers who'd driven his grandfather from the south that he would be back to correct their grammar — but it turns out to be the granddaughter, sewing "it in ink on the fabric of a myth," who has returned. Miss Anne better get used to the new Miss Dixie, who is, after all is said and done, her sister. (Sally Hemmings was Mrs. Jefferson's half-sister, a fact not often mentioned even in these days of DNA evidence of the foundering of our fathers and their foundlings, a fact that makes Jefferson's dalliances all the more Faulknerian, which is to say as American as, to return to Shockley's poem, "burning flags bearing crosses"). "you know me," the poem insists, "book away book away book away." We owe Myth Dixie to books and the flaming films made of them; we owe it to ourselves to look away, and looking back to what Al Jolson's blackface was covering over all that time. "aw aw aw mammy don't you want me don't you want me." (And by the way, none of these periods I'm closing these quotes with is in the poem; it's not that kind of period piece.) Shockley's poem lands her, and us, right back in "piedmont eden hell," but hell, I hear, is for heroes.

So, amongst heroes and hurricanes, we stumbled out of Miami, out of Oxford, into, to quote some Sun Ra, "other planes of there," and woke up with new songs in our ears. And on the next day we returned to the work.

Jeffery Renard Allen, photograph by Lynda Koolish

Jeffery Renard Allen

PRAYER TO ESHBU-ELEGBA

We have come
at the mercy of winds
We have come
at the mercy of sea
From the shackles of the old
to the shackles of the new

Caved
Cooned

Numb in the localized fist
Blind in the plastic order of the eyes

Ever-hooded
Empty-sleeved

A hollow people
drained of answers
marrow liquefied and drawn off
long black trail
ink from a pen

Men of reed
our scribes whistle

And the tongue takes odd turns
in the throat

Here
we kneel on broken ground
bent knees like arrows
We kneel and with heavy heads beat humble rhythm in dirt

Father
bend down and hit

Dance cools the town

Bright hands varnish drums in polished sound

They rise those who fell with
the dark tide
They rise those who fell with
setting sun/crushed beneath
They rise now with pierced glass sparkling in their knees

It is time to cut the cane

Father
remove the rag from the bush
When you dance on both feet
trouble ceases

March 29, 1999

HUNGER

Margins of season
I root here
where fire birds sing praises to the world
sun caked in wings

Fresh light splinters
the whole heart open and laid out
With sterile fingers I log dew
beads of my birth
Fat time
pounding at chest of
new day

I shout hard round names
slaughtered gods

Lines waver but they are not sea
Pitted words are not olives or stones
Bright pages lack the brilliance of flame in night

    Crooked smoke rises
branch on
branch
starry prize in eyes

Without let or hindrance
I recline
grass blade between teeth
green with glad force

Chant dry words
on dessicated tongue

When Lampaio calls
I will go

June 13, 2000

MUD WIT

for Olu Dara

Babygirl
get off my knee
ground need hoeing
Crack too high
Cane too bright
I kiss your buckled feet
Pen verses on Carolina tea labels
(Queen of kettle and spit)
There to witness
(Queensbridge)
Step off train
(Honey do)
guitar act like it don't know how to tune
(Do)
Caned in caroland
Clobbered with an Arkansas soupbone
in Tennessee
Sippi tree try to scare me be
hind its gray kudzu shawl
(I ain't getting)
Cat stole key to my bedroom door
Dog made me co-sign
White snake popped me on my left heel
Black snake shake shake its tail of fresh peas
Dead flower junky-nods over
the earth it has lost
I kneel to the buzzard
Bow to the crow
Mud comfort ain't no comfort at all
Rain shower
stir up this thick Mississippi blood

November 28, 1999 — April 4, 2002

DEEP ROCK

for L.

This hour of the star
we map our defense in
tall elephant grass
columns of stiff soldiers holding guard over a
hushed battlefield lumpy with bushels of snap corn and spud bean

Our village seiged
shade pressing in
houses framed in scissoring planes
and fanged faces lying in wait
Crops once layered
yield upon yield
thick as fresh paint
now laid waste
Amen
the sweaty hand of God
corn the only human touch

Sky drags her hem
sweeping a path of trace letters
we can't pronounce
music for anybody's tongue

Embrace your cello
curl into its ancient wood
time-thick vibrations
Set each speck of dirt circling in dance

Breathe
air sharp and perfect
sculpted by our chiseled lungs

Draw life from life
paradise angled at garden's edge

April 24 — May 18, 2001
New York/Nice/Paris/Los Angeles/New York

Wanda Coleman, photograph by Lynda Koolish

THREE-HEADED WOMON SONG

she put the whammy
on you
she say you a bald
headed
back stabber
she put the whammy on you
she say you
nevah rise above your
eyeballs
she put the whammy
on you. she
say your baby soul still doo-doo
in diapers
she put the whammy on you
she say
your kidneys are made of cheese
she put
the whammy on you. she say
when you
dead nuthin' happen
cuz you
don't rate a ghost

NOTES ON A DEPARTURE

after Jane Miller, for Jokie X Wilson

of the pains this indifferent Union
offers
i never thought I'd bear the weight
of a dying son — or the debt

when i was pregnant
birthing my child seemed a lovely loving
start to
life anew, not knowing love would not offset
poverty
not knowing art and desire would not
feed us
and dreams weren't enough to give
us all we'd soon desperately require

thirty-two years of struggle — the great price

late this afternoon, three years after
the scattering of ashes,
i found a poet's song among the sheets
of long-canceled accounts, the nude torsos
of muscular men and several clippings.

one reports the increased number
of weddings
of men to men, one male bride smiling at his groom
over glasses of champagne
we believe in god the caption shouts.
in yet another,
a dead dog returns to its owner, dripping
acid rain on the carpet.

another
describes the Pentagon's failure to test a possible cure
an infected actor undergoes religious conversion
a homosexual spy sues the FBI
a sailorboy is murdered under the fists
of five of his mates

among them i find
my son's paean to the god of fire
an ad for Eternity
the hospice admissions agreement
a photograph of a photograph of Marlene Dietrich
is our sexual and behavioral fate in our genes?
another caption asks

what has made
and kept us the freak children of the universe?

what evil says our deaths are deserved?

the California shore is along the ring of fire
where new earth forms
shaking loose the old, reminder to
the living —
nothing is solid or unshakable
to know blackness is to know bereavement
hence
the price/taxation for each blessed breath

as we tear at our hearts and our skins
as we grope among one another
among denials cruelties horrors
awestruck
and stumbling against the invisible

METAPHYSICALLY NIGGERISH

glimmerings of castrated history emerge from
a buried world thought lost
pried open by the swell & bloat of time
magnanimity in grace of psyche & soma
as within the groin spirits arise/darkest dark
strong mahogany wood
bursts of ancient stirrings
the release into firmament of the vortex named soul
gives back the sun
the armies of eternity bleed dry all flags
(Christian, free, English, still they say)
the hunger hidden in the tome erupts and
cracks the silent gray
a sweet death flows as secrets rain
and Africa rules Olympus

THE AFRICAN BENEATH THE AMERICAN

i speak like Plath after the oven did its job

these lines etched in slave-charred flesh
spoken crisply from noose-thickened lips

not a portrait, but a seared rendering
song forced through the throat that fights closing
gasps too painful to contain sentiment

like a smashed stolen grail under centuries of tarnish.

i write on my body. messages for seers.
nakedness as unconventional as foreign as
armed combat with enemies on these shores.

i strive because i must. i love out of spite. i pledge
my allegiance to a standard of ashes, embers and soot.
this is my anthem, a strident jig in the night

to that music beyond jazz

C. S. Giscombe, photograph by Lynda Koolish

C. S. Giscombe

THE BLACK RIVER

What am I missing?
Memory's a pleasure equal to any argument. I'm a nature boy, pleasure
me. We can vamp or we can essay and tote everything all at once.
A monster becomes terrifying to its maker, or something does.

* * *

Let's catch up. The Black River flows south into the Caribbean from the Santa Cruz
Mountains and on the tour of its lower part crocodiles approach the boat when the boatman
calls out their names: at the end of the tour's a low, narrow bridge and a woman selling food —
shrimp rolls, crab rolls — out of a small house. You eat and return.
What to believe? Push comes home to shove.
Situation's the uncertain argument: the neighborhood can't contain it
though it starts because of the neighborhood — cross it where you find it. One eats to stay on
the beam — finish that ice-cream fast before it melts, my feet
ate up the miles. The literature maintains itself way off, "more with a far-away voice."
Whites are semi-nude or nude all day in paradise. A dream of what?

* * *

The Black River tours are famous. Young unperturbed men stood in water
up to their waists as the boat passed, shrimp fishermen.
"Crocodiles only like the white meat," the boatman said.
Up and down the river it was an empire of reference! Love having been a slave right
here — lazy, industrious, the passion implicit in slave talk. We were with black tourists —
three young couples — from England, they were childless. Love stands in sometimes, love
goes to image like a monster when the load shifts. You know love.

* * *

I go toe to toe with nature. Sometimes I forget where
I am. Most days, upon our return from Jamaica,
the island was in my mind like a possession — back home one thing followed
another as though the path led to a zenith of human understanding.
To be equal's to fret like there was no more articulate tomorrow.

HOME AVENUE

The way home's left implicit, the beauty being to cause the same answer
to occur in every listener's mind so that she might enter the story at that point
on her own terms, so that she might bring her own terms to it. What
to come to! The story of the way in's intellectual property in that it does the work
property does for you, it articulates and re-states, it goes on ahead and appears
and re-appears when it's called.

* * *

Cincinnati's the border town — on its river, conventionalized — but Dayton's "like
the singing of Robeson." Home Avenue being a street winding across
black Dayton, neighborhood to neighborhood to neighborhood, no need to be
oblique here. Memory's meat on a bone.
There you are again, one might say. Who do you represent?

BALLAD VALUES (2)

I like "short grass" and the way we sang once — James Hamilton and I sang once — about liking meat that's close to the bone. And I prefer going over the junctions to being part of the argument. I like two buses rocking perilously close and metaphor judging you. I'm partial to ugly. I vary about the point where pleasure's a train of waves. I like how voice is a joke on passing and value the smooth as well as the sweet report. I like it once you get past the natural boundary. Lazy as I am I'd rather work in the sand than tire a singer.

LIGHT, BRIGHT, ETC.

Or skin's the *inevitable* appearance, the only castle, location only equaling voice. Skin meets the weave and you're clean; inland's no delta.

Skin's blank, though, and you can see it coming or going from far away. Neck to neck, side by side, a panoply of advantageous positions. Skin stands in; whole stories have to do with being caught up with on the road. Half-certain's different.

For the sake of argument, let image be the writhing end of hoop-la. I'm as interested as I should be. Let tomorrow come.

NEGROMANIA, NEGROPHILIA, NEGROPHOBIA

1.
Indianapolis on the q.t.: camp sites, no consequences. An argument would just single you out; my heart's empty, houses are empty too. Eating gives you coherence; music streaming by as though it was the fever of life.

2.
Indy's to the point where it's not paradise or hell but here you appear. (Bones show through, bones give out.) Argument only vexes a little bit. Shape's just patter to me, shape's got no door.

3.
Or Indianapolis is overstated, another hand — now you see it and then you don't. Between us — one articulate skin to the next — location's the temptation. I avoid pleasure like it was two dogs fighting over something.

4.
Any song would straighten you. The sum of the songs is you singing an "old" cover of the divine portent, you come to that

5.
in the doorway, under the little jaunty arch over the door they put on some Arts and Crafts houses in Indianapolis and other cities in the midwest and west instead of a porch. A telephone voice and a voice you can sin in. I'd be invisible if I wasn't so lazy. I'd be you and something else.

Terrance Hayes, photograph by Lynda Koolish

Terrance Hayes

MUTE TROUT

I swear a dim yellow light settled around the head
Of the little choir girl who'd stepped forward,
A red, extra large robe gushing over her shoulders,

To sing "More Like Jesus" and no one was moved.
Much later, I'm talking just before I died, I watched
A white boy slap the shit out of a man

Old enough to be his grandfather on the street
Outside my window and was happy, for a moment,
That two people could display such shamelessness,

Such a form of love. I knew God was there, probably
In the rain waiting patiently to drain into the small cracks
Between them, because the old man was breathless,

But not dead. We could not have been expected
To lift the holy girl into our arms, though she would have fit
Skinny as she was, light as the branch of a tree

In a river's current, light as driftwood,
Because what would her life have been like afterwards,
Shipped from pulpit to pulpit until she acquired a smell

Like newspaper swaddling though months
Of rainfall on the steps of an abandoned house?
I would have yelled, *Hey, cut that shit out!*

But my window was shut, the street almost empty
When I stepped outside like a man of God.
Who can live like that? To the girl I wanted to say,

Wear that song out, Baby. Break me down.
I was never going to be not thinking of her
The way a man following his future down the street

Is never not thinking. I wanted to say, *You are the money*
I left behind, the money I lost, the money stolen from me.
When I left home I found leaves and the strangers

I knew would be there, and all through those blocks:
Want blossoming at the corners of my mouth.
One of them died, I know, or would somewhere

With that guilt that is truly the door to redemption.
It was as if they had no bodies. And when I reached
Toward them, it was as if the air rose and settled

Like skin that had been burned and healed improperly,
Or like wet gauze waiting to be removed...
Are you here to hear the story of the mute trout?

How God gave them voices filled with water?
How we creatures of the open land lived
Trying to make the air sing, but our lyrics were more

Like rocks and knuckles than lyrics? I called out
To the old man who'd risen and walked away and the air,
I swear, formed a song like that. There was nothing

To do except look backwards. They'd left the path
And I hadn't noticed when I stepped outside.
But I knew the rest of the world was trying to sing

Because I couldn't breathe. Church, let's make it up.
Who believes the air can consume a song?
Who believes our music does not float inevitably free?

OHIO RIVER REGION

My wife pokes fun at the way I say pencil & Pennsylvania
    & I at the way she says syrup with no *sir* in the syrup
Being born as she was, Midwestern & almost Southern

    Just a few fish from Covington, Kentucky where they say
Everyone is a close cousin & the Justice of the Peace
    Looks the other way because the street his office window

Looks on would be just a one way alley in big cities,
    But not in this town which would be a city only if Cincinnati
        sank
Into the Ohio River along with the ghosts of King Records,

    Bootsy Collins & all those police-battered blacks —
They pray for it: the covetous Covingtonians, the J.O.P.
    & his vague, small-mouthed wife —

She would have been a valedictorian were she not a Born-Again
    & born instead when I was born & a little bit smarter,
She might know it if she knew me, the one her husband calls

    Tall Ticketed Black Boy Looking For A Break Between The Shotgun
Wedding Of Smith To Smith,
            "I saw him," the J.O.P. says
    "When I looked to the window, you need to dust the blinds by
        the way,

& could not see the street or Mr. Bob with his broom-
    Handle mustache because that boy's egg head blocked my view,
I don't want to marry Smith to Smith, truth be told,

    Keeping their bad luck blood in the same bad blood like a river

Shaped like an O, where does the Ohio go, Baby Girl,
    & where does it come from, once I tried swimming away

From you & your beer-battered fish, but did nothing more than a
    clock
        Does, my hands too small to gather more than the debris
Of sewers along the way, but I marry them year in & out

    Because love knows nothing but love same as stupid, this fish,
        Girl,
Makes me sadder than a Hell's Angel, I can taste one hundred miles
    in the meat."

NOTHING

which is what the first idiot says
to the second idiot in the joke
I have made up but will not share with you

when the scent of another of those saltless,
full boned marital truths hovers in the air
between us. I feel the joke

knock around and expand in my gut,
pushing all the good air out.
I'd rather be a blind girl, Etta James sings

in the jukebox playing inside my brain
and no one is willing to eat or dance
because everyone is sleeping

in my heart's grand hotel:

my single breasted mother in her soft blue
shirt, and *Don't Explain* begging

on the jukebox in my father's skull
where he dances his soft shoe blues.
I love the way a good song makes you

say nothing. And I believe success
and happiness is not the same thing.
I feel the joke walk in ahead of us

when we enter your parents' house
where the big bed fills the bedroom
and the big tv fills the den and the Sundays

are filled with *Amen*. Sometimes
when we are sitting with our heads bowed
over dinner I can hear nothing:

not God saying you are blessed,
not the meat cooling, not your parents'
nor our own breathing. I love the way love

makes us say nothing like a good song,
but I believe it could be fear. I remember lying
on my belly in the darkness, my cheek

to the pillow, my head to the wall
on our marriage night in that grand hotel,
you waiting and me saying it to you.

Kim Hunter, photograph by Lynda Koolish

Kim Hunter

accident in a naked place

there are three
there is one
there is chance

what mask are these words
for what will come
your voice rides the low cotton sky
spreads water and light
but nothing grows

it happens again
and a faint scratch
comes like lightning
the relief of fire in the dry places
the next time the same
and we realize
how empty gifts can be

mirror greetings pass
faces on the street
fine how are you shields
to pretend we pass like time
instead of in it

three one chance
something to one
what time is it in there
i'll never forget
ol' what's his name
because he'll come up next time
right

yes well everyone has an excuse
tales of clowns stepping over the people
as they storm the castle
heads and necks underfoot
clowns without paint
bogart their way to royalty
wigs and big shoes

then the stories of torches
to be carried in the aforementioned
castle storming
torches wet and unlit for years
and it's all true

the clowns are paid off
the clouds are seeded with money
we have paid to watch someone else's dreams
with no choices to breathe for
we do not sleep or wake
but hover between blank illuminated screens
ground mirror fragments of the corporation
the body that can't be pursued

with machines the metal crunches
and sometimes there is blood
with people there are children
and there is always blood
glasses fall
bridges give way
light burst from the sky
to a spot no one could have guessed

and mysteries in the open
seem like open mysteries

set us to reaching behind the numbers
that were supposed to tell us
something
set us to dismember the calculation
the schedule
the umbrella that fits
in the briefcase that is always
with us
the alarm on the birthday clock
with the ready made roses
in the store where they can't forget
our names
but never know
who we are

fine how's the weather
thanks that's a shame
and you

i worked on race at the factory

race is an invention
i worked on race at the factory
and class
and the clothes coded for our sex organs
to shield and signal
from layers and layers the deepest

factories are good places for things
to come out one like the other
money and city limits read at night

help children sleep
as for dreams
they are on their own

if someone were not white
the blood on the field would
still be red just not as much
and the bones that fertilize
the cotton plant
and the bones that trail the tears
and the bones that jump
out of the factory window
with hair and sweat burning
could not be made up

so we are stuck with our history
with lips pursed over jello
and nervous young cops
guns un-holstered at night
after the school burns down

bullets arrive in the brain
through the television set by accident
but chances are your skin
the same as the skin of the womb you knew
is a magnet
for dead places in the city
fantastic dead places
that we can read about
as for dreams
they are on their own

no like place

the air and cement here are stained
with good intentions
with intentions
are stained

postage stamp patches of green
are covered with a fast drying mix
on sale till friday

they make the gunfights everywhere
and ship them here special
in exchange for the factory jobs
in exchange for having no factory
in place of the hole

the humidity is a blanket sack
over the face in a sauna
they predict thunder but no storm
the tears just won't fall

i pass someone i know
waiting for the bus
she waves back to me
her hand in front of her face
as if she is warding off evil spirits
or paparazzi

it has a name
they had to call it something
even if they didn't know
what it meant

it means hold
this till i say let go
it means get up
i don't care what time it is
it is a question of food
not where it grows
but how you get it
and the chopping noise
of the raggedy mechanical blade
that separates those questions
at the neck

* * *

actually there are two horses
but one is at the pawn shop
we thought there were three
but one was a rat on stilts
trying to get a job
with the mounted police
on belle isle
it's all about uplift

in real life the one
that has not been stolen
for meat and parts
has a minimum wage
armed guard
who has trouble staying
out of mcdonald's
even after his cousin's funeral

there used to be more
before the museum

bought them and charged us
for looking

now you have to go
to the barbershop
or wait on the steps
after services to hear
what it was like
in the good old days

my father told me
how the white people
in the shoe store
would try to guess his size
because once he tried them on
the shoes were his
fit or not

Honorée Fanonne Jeffers, photograph by Lynda Koolish

Honorée Fanonne Jeffers

PHILLY IN THE LIGHT

for Hayes

Y'all carry weapons up here
in the grocery stores? I ask
the security guard at the corner
SuperFresh. He's bagging fruit for me,
and there's a gun on his hip. If I
weren't such a Southern Belle,
I'd say right to his face, *That's a mighty*
big piece you're carrying. I'd make my voice
deliberately corn pone and molasses
and he'd laugh, charmed by my
ignorance of the Great Migration pace.

I am an Eve in this northern garden
where trash planted one night
sprouts ghettos the next morning.
Where they dropped fire on a whole
city block, watched the chickens, goats,
people burn all day long on television.
They smelled cooking flesh
in the air and called it barbecue.
I shake my head at these city dwellers
who don't know that killing should
be done in private, never for open
eyes or in the light.
This is a lesson that even the children
of the South have learned.

ANOTHER EASTER POEM

Mary had a baby...
What did she name him?
— *Traditional spiritual*

I think, too late for me now
in this thirty-fifth year.
Perhaps my body would comply,
but the fears of a child, my weakness,
would come roosting again.
I'll never be that sky-sent woman alone
in her task, a pair of hands sewing
my son's death robe. A mother,
chained as saint, shouting out
loud the disorder of faith.
Knees wide open, no freedom
from the Spirit's battering ram.

Now my belly is rounded out with disuse.
What you gone name
Now my hands cup under this dusty womb.
What you gone name
Not even death curled up in here,
but salt spilling, phantom,
and my dream's neck snapped.
What you gone name

How could I justify the third morning anyway,
my own blood's blood as wine?
How could I roll back the stone
to dam a goddamned grief?
What you gone name that pretty little baby?
Maybe I would have called him
man, prayer, bread.

INSTRUCTIONS FOR ACADEMIC POETS WHO TALK TO GOD

Don't say you know poems are scripture
chiseled in blues,
visions of a certain lunatic,

ignore God laughing in your ear
at the question about *necessary inspiration,*
and don't you tell your students or your colleagues

that you pray. — What are you, crazy?
You can say you have been listening
closely to the spirituals since graduate school

but deny those are a part of God, too.
Instead, discuss in a scholarly fashion
Marian Anderson, Paul Robeson

or the Fisk Jubilee Singers (please
be aware mentioning Mahalia Jackson's
shouts might trip you up), and remember

not to linger on the faith of those slaves
who composed the songs in the first place,
just how they got over in the midst of chaos.

Pretend you aren't the best of the sad
red clay you were formed from,
holy spit mixed into the bones.

Think quick.
Talk in your best clipped, nasal
accent about *nuance, resonance,*

perhaps *confession*
but don't expound too much on pain.

TUSCALOOSA: RIVERSONG

for Mister Weaver

1. *Black Warrior speaks*

The night before they came,
I walked on my river. I had strange
dreams: bloody shouts to the sun,
bodies in the trees, twirling legless.
I sang until morning. I sang, and the white
ones were here sniffing an empty breast.
They are here but I cannot die.
My tribe is strong behind our
drums and sliced trees.
We are strong against these whites
with sticks like dirty breath, these
silly children snatching toys.
They do not see me.
My tongue is strong and hides me.
I cannot die. They do not see me
walking on my river, my teeth biting
at early chains. They only
know they choke on my songs.

2. *DeSoto speaks*

I have seen him before all
over the world. This Indian,
this Tuscaloosa, this red man
with the black name dares
to think he will defeat me
and my tribe. Who is he to imagine
he will kill me with his songs,

sacred or commonplace?
Who is he to be sure that his spirits
will hear, float down this river,
sting the skin of slaves?
I am the one who cries the music
of God, and Tuscaloosa is mine.
He cannot live past my morning
into night. I want his seed to die
in this water. I want his mouth
wounded with slime.

Tuscaloosa.
I will push him into that river,
this warrior of a cracked womb.
His song will never be earth or flesh.

3.

Tuscaloosa sleeps in the water
stirs the silt of blues
makes music of ashes
feeds death clotted anger

Tuscaloosa sleeps in the water
sucks gore from his lungs
strips the green crucifix
roars the gumbo scream

Tuscaloosa
Tuscaloosa
Tuscaloosa

Trane's *Alabama*
a Creole agony

blood slung through air
a throat-filled epiphany
death licking madness
an elegy for mud

4.

This is the river of no longer.
Here by the side of the Black Warrior,
lights are woven through branches.
Water level signs hang from the trees:
1919 1857 1913 1989 and on.
A memory of what is no longer
painful. From year to year
the levels of the water climb
higher than before, and in the spring
the people of town visit
mounds filled with bones.
They buy feathers and skin painted
bright colors, or whistles drilled
with holes that make sounds
of animals unnecessary and small.

No one talks of the year he died.
Tuscaloosa is a river, a place
where quiet blood is shed.
Tuscaloosa is a river, signs
nailed to trees. We do not speak
in old tongues. We blow pretty
noises through holes.

5.

Tuscaloosa
This is not the river, so long,

so wide, Hayden's water, baptism
of survival. The river that Mama
and I crossed over one summer,
crossed over history's concrete
back, the river that made her ask,
Do you think we should pray I can't
see the shore this is the river the slaves
had to cross oh God I can't see
the shore do you think we should pray?
This is not Jordan, only the river
DeSoto tossed three hundred souls into,
watched the water grow tall
as they squirmed like dancing
stones, watched the water dark
and struggling rise and rise,
bubbles blowing from the children's
mouths, mother's wet chants
swallowed by dirt.
This is not Jordan.
There is no milk and honey
waiting on the other side, only
dead stones flat and smooth.
This is not Jordan, only simple water
muddied from a season of rain.
This is not Jordan, but I have
prayed at this shore anyway.

6.

Tuscaloosa
feathered with spirit
red libation on the tongue
claws mystery into earth
scatters song on this river

Tuscaloosa
prayer of ancient thirst
wind through clenched fist
claws mystery into earth
scatters song on this river

Tuscaloosa
holy man swept into light
gnarled root of God
claws mystery into earth
scatters song on this river

Tuscaloosa
Tuscaloosa
Tuscaloosa

dark arms cup the blade
blue spit in the scripture's eye
do not walk across my water
do this in remembrance of me

Nathaniel Mackey, photograph by Lynda Koolish

Nathaniel Mackey

SONG OF THE ANDOUMBOULOU: 58

The intractable two no longer among
us, he her ecstatic exegete, wishing
the world away, nose between her
legs as in a book… Comes up for
air.
She straddles his lap. A stiff bouquet
opens their noses… Not that it
would ever not be there, not that,
even so, it would be the same. Animal
grace fallen down or away from,
all
for naught if not amended, made of its
own
remit. A lit screen showed it was us
rubbed away, Dread Lakes' namesake
brew, drank our fill, poppin fell from
the sky… Oddly fed. Feasted on
grief.
Debris bumped our heads, rubble
hurt our feet. Fingerless, if not
without hands, drew back from
reaching,
Nub the new kingdom come…

Remnant light lay weakening light's
retreat, children said to be of the night no
longer children, such what we'd have
otherwise been… Somewhere someone
chanted,
an echo we looped and relooped. Dub it

was as much as it was Nub we were
in, ersatz eternity looped ad infinitum,
loop
given reverb to. Echoes flew close to the
earth, bleak reconnaissance. Tape ran
away in reverse, took us with it, beginning
to be alive it seemed... We whose two
demanded a longer count long since
riven,
I was only what was left. She his unim-
pressed interpreter, I thought, bone as
well as body looked at, leafed, eyes lit
like
ember, book of no turning
back

•

Back seemed all there was, alive
begun to appear to be ember, interregnum,
deathroll exception, proof... Terrain
like no other, nubscape. Flags
filled
up the sky... Two loomed incalculable,
aggregate regress, Nub's raw republic
absconded with we thought, Nub short
for Nubia we thought, thought we
thought,
there no more the where we'd have been...
Such that one, being what was left,
blew up, an eye before that a blind
lemon,
blue lemon, teardrop adjournment,

salt… So that everything it took took
wing, newly adduced or indifferent, no
one to say which, well-paved outskirts
of Nudge notwithstanding, Nub's new
landing
point. Armless, one lay in wait, moot
warrior, crouched behind a bush put upon
by wind, misgiving, doubt… There
that we'd have otherwise been, blue
summit, state stand only as we'd allow.
Lovers'
dub covered lovers' republic. Something
obscene, it seemed, was on the box…
Crawled on our stomachs, elbows to
dirt. "The Inch Worm" was on the
box…
The box filled with water, dry rot,
worm
routes voices ran
thru

Wrung water from a sawed-off branch,
coaxed omen. Hollowed-out tree trunk
thumped… So much easier said
so much of what we said, rhythm
log
wasted by ant wing, worm jaw,
balafon
bridge undone. Scrounged around
among bushes and tree roots. Went to
rise but our heads held us down…
We were Andoumboulou, bloated
heads atop shrunken bodies, the
song
said to be ours a repeating head's
vamp-till-ready, torn heads' mended
spin. Shrunken bodies, bloated heads,
we
were Andoumboulou, bodies more
head than husk were song body, torn
heads'
compromise

•

Rummaged around on all fours to
bug accompaniment. What we wanted
we couldn't have. Multiple the
names it went by, legion, wars
over
which one fit broke out, nation of
none though we were… Not yet
nation of Nub that we were, said to've
been born with barbs in our skin,
anaesthetic nation of Nuh… Said
to've
been born in beds made of glass,
"Bed,
be our balafon bridge," we exhorted,
"bed, be our rhythm log." Glass meant
broken, slivers where we lay, ythmic
digestion
held even so, shards bone-deep it
meant… Bridge meant see-thru,
sayless, something we'd assume
so elliptical it seemed, unsay said it
best… Unsay said what there was of
it
to say. Nub's low skyline lay to our
left…
Nub lay close to the earth… Nub cut us
off. We were never all there. Raw knuckles
pounding the dirt bled rivers. Bloodrun
carried
us away

•

Scrounged around on what earth was
left, the intransigent few Nub stubbed
its toe on. All of earth was what
earth was left so few we were, back
at
some beginning it seemed... It was
morning, gray morning, pearl divers
chanting in the Gulf beside the
bed, clock dial phosphorescent, lit.
The lovers lay again without
recoil,
world without war without end
intimated, dream they'd awaken
from... In a ship's hold helpless,
hair
the look of thicket, ship of state they'd
call
it, crushed... But for now, before that,
sleep of ages, again as if starting
from scratch. Asleep yet on the tips of
their
tongues kept asking, salt not known to
call itself
salty, what to
say

What of us wouldn't carry caught
on the bank of the river, lit spear
brandished on the bank of the
river, lit spear hoisted, flung…
Locked

and braided eldren sang without
sound, sang without voice with
what blood laid claim to… Blood
was a paperthin slick atop water.
Water

ran where voices would've been…

Blood spoke in tongues from the
far side of tongues. Bed be none
of the above, blood admonished,
unsay's

day if not begun
soon
come

SONG OF THE ANDOUMBOULOU: 62

Cement sky we were slow to get
going under. Indigent wish for an
alternate world run out. Flat rock
skipped on water… The low-lying
sky
pressed our heads flat, Operation
Spin, teeth clenched, our heads
went round and round. I shivered
and shook, finally caught myself,
hunched-up shoulders no match
for
the wind, an ill wind we'd heard,
which
it was… "Lay low lie," we lip-sync'd,
salaam'd. Peace be with us we
begged. Operation Kill was afoot,
we were on the run, ran standing
still,
paralytic dream come true. Air's
forfeiture it seemed, we with an
ear for asthmatic flutes, cement
sky progeny, tribe of late repute,
beyond only more of the same…

The new day dawned as gray as
any. Low sky, low ceiling we
stood bent over by, a cold wind
blew in off the bay… So it
was
and so it went. In cement sky
country we ate cement soup,

Operation Grab the law of the
land…
Bread we broke with hammers.
Crust cut our gums. In cement sky
country we coughed, cleared our
throats…
Words were at a premium…
Hemmed and
huffed

•

Planes flew… Bombs fell…
Operation Boast. Operation Lie.
Thug regime scrimmaging thug
regime, we were in the middle.
My
head was a flat rock the size
of a silver dollar. The others'
all were
as well… Operation Spin skipped
our heads across water, thin rocks
glancing the face of the water, the
Dread Lakes eldren were back. A
certain
us, a certain them they related…
Good's good war against bad they
were pushing, talking the two
again…
It was Kali's time, flat rocks a
necklace round her neck, heads
crushed flat, slab sky… We were
tramping, trudging, trying to make

heaven, stuck feet mashing the
spot
we walked circles in, paralytic
dream's repeat. Ripped ring
shout, paralytic dream's unend,
earth
we receded from… Dwelled on high,
low
sky notwithstanding. No part of it…
Nothing to do with us… Operation
Gloat. Operation Slaughter. Name
after name after name… Not in ours
we
said, slapped heads ringing, not
to be Andoumboulou again. *Not to*
be Andoumboulou again but were, we
within we athwart we ad infinitum,
voice we were chided by. Bottom
voice,
low sky's amanuensis… Low sky, slow
start, we staggered, stood our ground…
Home at last, it said. We laughed…
Jaws
tight, teeth clenched, we circled. Words poured
out like sweat… Bullets flew, legs bent,
buckled.

Square one. Square
less than
one

•

It was the Ricochet Lounge
we ducked into, last call.
Sun Ra played a Toupouri
harvest. "They plan to leave,"
we
semisaid, semisang, chimed in.
Hoarse arkestral flutes laid a
rug of water under our feet.
It was the end of the world
again...
A warning song the semisong we
sang,
we all walked circles inside our
heads. Each of our heads an
aroused ark, a flat rock we
rode,
we awoke aboard ship, a spinning
rock flying saucerlike, obduracy's
day drawn out. Dread auspice's day
a skipping rock we grew wet with,
pant
legs and hemlines wrinkling the face
of the bay, at obduracy's behest we
walked on water... Stone ark we
stepped and stood on, miraculously
flat, spun with, could barely keep our
feet...

Obdurate sky the it we sensed wrote
epitaphs on, we without world or
it without us, circling square less

than one, centrifugal, farther out
                                        the
  longer we walked. Choked up
 wearing epic shirts, moot ribbons,
    ythm's day begun… We were
   he's and we were she's, each
  one or the other, felt between our
                                           legs
divining which. Home where there was
   none, stone as close as we got,
  talking the twos again… We were
    I and I, each I another, felt among
   ourselves fathoming which… One
                                             was
  dreaming again, lost to us dreaming,
                                               dream-
ing us lost
again

•

If I stood I stood in line like
everyone else. A lone pigeon
pea lay on my plate... Growls,
gruff stomach. Polyphysite
cry...
Hell was holding elections
again...
Breastbone would be our pillow,
Kali flatchested of late. Stuffed
her bra with the rocks our
heads were, were she to wear a
bra...
We stood in line waiting to skip
our heads across water. We stood
in line, each awaiting our turn. We
stood in a straight line, an unwound
circle,
our own heads between finger
and thumb as if ours to throw, we
stood on the shore at the bay
skipping stones or we stood on the river
bank up from the bay skipping
stones.
Water and sky were one I wanted to
say... We stood on the shore at the bay
harvesting rocks or we stood on the
river bank up from the bay harvesting
rocks.
The river ran to the bay... One was
everyone within, all in one I wanted
to say, graced moment gone away from

again come back again, back but a
wisp
of itself, ghost moment, proof it lay
else-
where,
prod

Tracie Morris, photograph by Lynda Koolish

Tracie Morris

APOLOGY TO PANGEA

I seent you
blue: silk on a peacock feathered eyelet
corona around pupil of the old
Dye with expensive tastes:
red — corpuscles of the dyers.
In the underbelly of current,
coffin canoes heavily down.

And here we be with capes, spandex and big hair
hieroglyphs spelling *superduper*, people who made atoms,
his momma, molecules before mourning.
Dat was me with the buck dance and chicken head.
Me, making Grits gris-gris, wif.
Can I say sorry for dem sweep yo feet, Mam?
Do I throw coarse salt over ma shoulder?

from THE MYOMECTOMY CYCLE

4. Body full of blood
hold it — a cradle
You rock back&forth
in cramp. A slave ship?
A deep blue? fibrous rope but/knot
umbilical. Blub, blub.

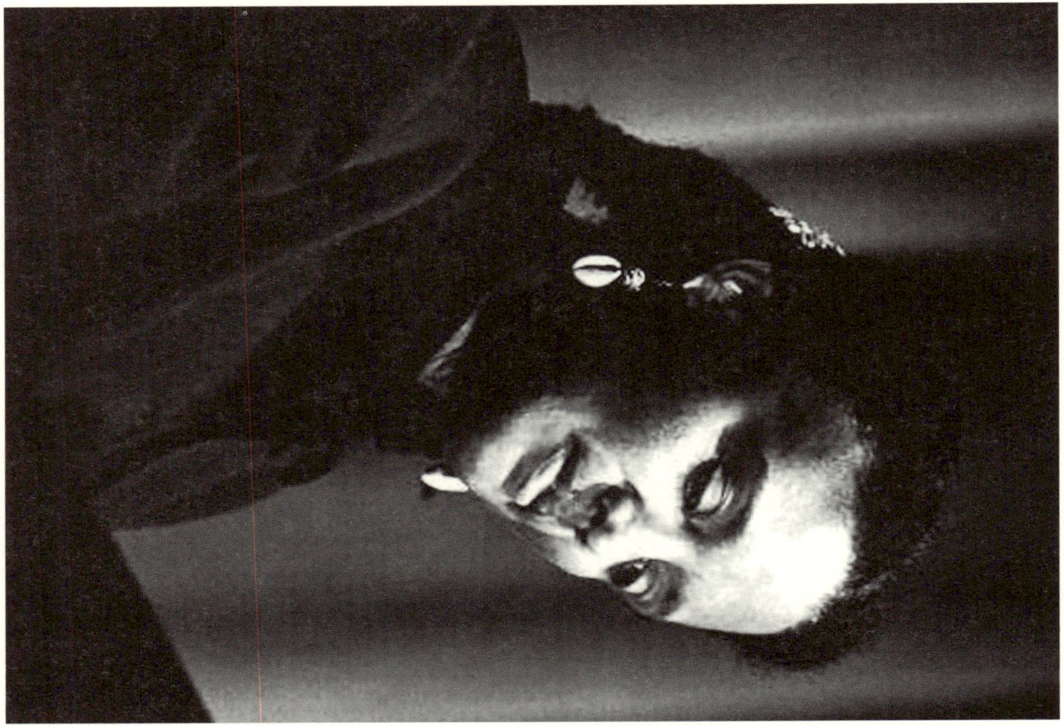

Harryette Mullen, photograph by Lynda Koolish

UNACKNOWLEDGED LEGISLATOR

After singing the final page
the poet passes out
ceremonial pens.

As the poem is sighed into law
rules to be made are broken
and broken rules amended.

When the archival papers
are all singed in blood
the poet's meter expires.

HEADLINES

1. Fired cook was deranged.
2. Baldheaded woman's distressed.
3. Flypaper gets inspected.
4. Trial lawyers' profession distorted.
5. Balloonist disgusted, round-the-world trip falls flat.
6. Kiwis, these birds are unflappable.
7. Obese sheep distended.
8. Madonna disguised in convent.
9. Jockey to be debriefed shortly.
10. Las Vegas delighted to conserve power.

BUMPER TO BUMPER

I'd rather be at the beach. I'd rather beat each ache. I'd rather be a dirty blond than a clean-cut brunet. If I had to choose between being richer or smarter, I'd rather have the money because I'm smart enough already.

I'd rather not think about it. I'd rather not go into that. I voted but I'd rather not say which one I punched. I'd rather switch than fight. I trust my psychic friend over Dan Rather.

I'm stuck in traffic when I'd rather be surfing. My other car is the Metro, *mi otro carro es El Metro*. I'd rather drive than walk. I'd rather work than starve. I'd rather drink unfiltered tap water and sleep on a lumpy futon than live anywhere else in this godforsaken world.

#6 SEPULVEDA

Arrival at terminal laxative. In and out with fries. Fox mauls hill. A colored crowd. Sad cactus left over from family nursery's going out of business sale. The drive-in movie was a used car lot, then a flea market, now it's condos. *Botanica* across from coffee shop near Cuban restaurant where workers gather for lunch. A few blocks down, you can get five different *mole salsas* and wire dollars to Oaxaca. At pancake palace I hop on the bus across from all night news guy. Today's special veggie burger at Hot Diggity, home of the Y2K dog. Turn right past blank soldier and bland sailor. A white cross for each life lost. Pencils, toothpicks, chopsticks. Trees in this wood, all cut down to size. Pay a large sum for a large bag of popcorn. End of the line, everyone out. Grab a *Daily Bruin* and run. It's okay, the crazy people on the bus aren't talking to themselves. They're speaking on their cell phones.

BROKEN GLISH

(inverse translation of a sonnet by Pablo Neruda)

Finding myself in the desert, I planted a luminous seed. I let go a howl past moist teeth, certain it couldn't have been the mute sunshine laughing, a sane cello, or a brand new brain. No one came near. Nor was I ever shallow or newsworthy to you, as the moon has revealed. Only a murmur blasted by brief springs, by the dry impenetrable glare of a taproot. I fell asleep on rational sand dunes, where the cactus rasped above my toenails, a solid stench descending from oblivion. Slowly, unlike the spines I was stuck with, I spoke calmly, addressing the watery ocean I'd discovered in my dotage — and I went on undeterred, healed by that unwavering stink.

DRINKING MOJITOS IN CUBA LIBRE

"My mojito in La Bodeguita. My daiquiri in El Floridita." A postcard of fidelity shaking hands with earnest money. Lost in the streets of Havana, gasping for breath *como un pez sin agua.* As hot as it is, as black as can be, as dark as this combustible star. *Sí, hace calor, pero* only *turistas* wear big brims or ultraviolet lenses. You hot, you thirsty? You buy us mojitos? You bring your *yanqui dolor.* We show our splendid squalor. Milk for baby, you give me dollar. You black, we black. See my scar from the war in Angola. Still working for a Cuba libre. Tropicola's sweeter than Coke. Mix rum and sugar with sweat of a slave. We work for pesos and beg for your stinking dollar. I'll show you where Hemingway wrote, the bar where he sipped his swizzle. You'll owe me a mojito. *Que se vayan los gusanos.* Crush with a pestle. Add rumba. Stir briskly with a drop of African blood.

MERMAID OF PALMARES

In a mythical Palmares
between Ocean and Palms,
a marooned mermaid
sings a samba in the shower.

On a landlocked traffic island
at a gridlocked intersection, deafened by sirens,
a dreadlocked mermaid parks her bike
and opens a bottle of sparkling water.

One night when earth shakes
and rocks her bed from side to side,
a drowsy mermaid awakes from her dream
of sailing on a stormy sea.

EL MALECÓN

How many engineers trained to hold back a million
  gallons of ocean *en El Malecón?*
How many cars speeding *en El Malecón?*
How many couples kissing *en El Malecón?*
How many poor folk fishing for a living *en El Malecón?*
How many poot-butt buses *en El Malecón?*
How many hustlers hustling *en El Malecón?*
How many male, female, and she-male cons
  en El Malecón?
How many tourist taxis *en El Malecón?*
How many Mafia nostalgia hotels *en El Malecón?*
How many sexy school girls *en El Malecón?*
How many mermaids on shore leave *en El Malecón?*
How many collisions and breakdowns *en El Malecón?*
How many starving dogs with ribs like xylophones
  en El Malecón?
How many khaki cops with clean guns *en El Malecón?*

Vista del mar en el Malecón,
Where the guard warns us to move along,
because we're black?
Because he thinks we're prostitutes? Or spies?
Because we might throw a bomb?
Just because we don't belong?
Or he's afraid we'll clone a cyclone
aquí en El Malecón?

Mendi Lewis Obadike, photograph by Lynda Koolish

Mendi Lewis Obadike

FIFTEEN

for Stephen

Faced with his jaw, his cocked head, the stubble
On his jutting chin, you might believe
He is all points. Even the thick shock
Of hair that used to roam his head is now oiled
And stretched and woven into tight rows.
You could almost forget his naps.
Like most things intimate, he buries
Them close to his body. He even guards
His words with teeth and slightly cracked lips.

Sometimes, I find myself tricked,
As if I never watched him practice this stance.
Two years ago, he measured each risk
Of fashion and gesture by an older cousin's
Calculations. Now, sparsity is a sixth sense.
To catch him feeling, you have to know
The glint in his eye is a smile. Notice,
When you hug him, how he holds on
Longer than you. But give up
On full sentences and eye contact.

This is fifteen.

Wait for him on the other side
Of hardness.

PROTEST POEM

Should the years continue to press
As they press now, and in their pressing,
Press the sugar from my skin, let
The stone that forms inside me
Be amber.

Should there be aching, then,
For sweetness, should they
Come looking and find me, let them
Find in me this rock, and not
My bitter carapace. This rock,
And think of honey, stored away
For safe-keeping.

Tomorrow, who knows?

Should the sun burn out,
As it plans to do, and as it burns,
Burn down all the trees, let
My shadow be a cool thing,
Reaching out to shade you.

TRADITION/ABSTRACTION

after Gilberto Gil

I met this girl who was visiting Atlanta. She looked
So sweet. She went around with this tough girl,
This very smart girl. So tough, she walked alone
At night. So smart, no one ever bothered her.

She walked with a wide gait and always looked people in the eye.
Singing sometimes. Sometimes just thinking. I met this girl
In Atlanta who looked sweet. She was visiting. This was when
Tribe was still together, before Tupac and Biggie got killed.

This was when we still protested Freaknik. Sometimes singing.
I met this girl in Atlanta at a party in a church on the corner
Of JP Brawley before the library "Club Woody." "Club Woody"
Because you could meet people there.

Sometimes in the stacks. Sometimes in the carrels.
Everyone else, that is, not me. This was right after
They beat the students on MLK. This was right when
I started to get jaded. Jaded, but still I believed

This girl's sweet way, visiting Atlanta. Her way was so sweet,
It made her friend sweet. Her friend who was so tough and so smart,
Walking down any street alone at night, looking them in the eye.
Singing. Or just thinking. Everyone else, that is. Everyone else.

Sometimes, visiting Atlanta, I met this girl. Her friend,
She walked, just singing. Think so smart. Night right sweet.
Just one them. This was no bother, believe. Every eye, that is,
Not alone. Looking street in the way. Girl. Some tough else.

James Richardson, photograph by Lynda Koolish

James Richardson

PARNASSUS RISING

I. Urania, muse of heavenly inspiration

Pentecostal flames
singe the page at 3am:
Holy Ghost at work

II. Polyhymnia, muse of sacred poetry

Vowels undulate
right to left in golden script;
ululations soar.

III. Terpsichore, muse of dancing

Sun spills on wood floor
dust flecks — charmed — spiral-waltz up,
greet their lofty lord.

IV. Calliope, muse of epic poetry

Rappers slice airwaves,
sword-fight AM/FM haze:
afroed Beowulves

V. Clio, muse of history

brown virginia grass
froth-white with autumn-dawn dew:
satchels... briefcases

VI. Melpomene, muse of tragedy

Dagger you've become,
spreading pain in whorls of red:
splinter in my thumb.

VII. Thalia, muse of comedy

Streams tickle my tongue
Pillow clouds tease my eyelash
Foot slips in sheep shit.

VIII. Erato, muse of love poetry

Nether-knife of flesh
heat emits from bushy tufts —
tongue and thumb draw sap

IX. Euterpe, muse of music and giver of pleasure

Flute breath woos your neck
each hair trembles, genuflects:
Who's your daddy now?

J-O-Y

for JF

I. "*J* means Jesus first."

The spit-cup
by the pantry door
that holds wet snuff,
profound tobacco juice,
knows spring comes only
under cover of clouds
or cover of nights wild
with winds, cold rains.
In a desperate hoax, you
conjure those mornings
tender with greens
a kind, tepid sun,
a sky overwhelmed
with the very blue found
on a Rice Krispies box.
Artifice, then, becomes
the god-archetype that
masters every burgeoning
madrigal, symphony, aria,
sonnet, paean, or villanelle
to meadows, pastures, siskins' wings.
And you, the requisite
pretty thing, had better
not disturb the groove
that never asks that love
be proved: old sheets
with hymen blood procure
a wedding ring.

II. "*O* means Others second."

The crumbs by the TV stand,
loyal to every pitiful heave,
harden in the sunlight
or take their leave when air
from an angry forceful door
slams shut, and you are left
to breathe dishwater suds,
the faintest aftershave.
These are the same crumbs,
mute and blind, that drink
the odors, poised, contrived
from ipecac, hot tea, Ex-Lax;
midmorning finds
your angst appeased, doused
with Camay and Pepsodent.
Cross-legged on the sofa
in a pink chemise,
you are loved by a cat,
a pink, sleeping child;
and while bits of puke
tease your throat like gauze,
leaves sun-shimmer in midair
like talkshow applause:
the cow vomits its cud;
it's chewed a bitter thing.

III. "*Y* means Yourself last."

Huddle your passions in
an unswept place beyond
the intrigues of April sun;
consider the baby's spitup

an epiphanal grace;
hum TV commercials;
get your housework done.
And muse on your fortunes,
the greenest of joys, greener
than an Apple Jacks box:
a well-tempered house,
a charming pink spouse
who has let your momma —
no, mother — live with you.
The good woman splendors
in a nurse-watched room,
cozy in her piss, blissfully
drooling snuff. You author
these fortunes and thank
the good Lord for good
English, good hair, light skin,
and wit. So what if
on some nights he comes
home to his suburban lair
martini-maddened?
He's ravenous for you,
forces it from behind.
Coos to you hotly:
Come on, Elondra,
don't be stiff; jive it, jive it;
you don't have to BE white.
But back to this present,
to this household, this joy:
You tiptoe past the room
with the woman whose hair
is gray and fast balding,
whose brain is now feathers
random and disheveled,

who sometimes, says the nurse,
rasps out *Lonnie Mae...*
And onward, onward to
the pink, sleeping child;
though his lips fill too full,
his hair rages blond.
You finger the coolness
of your brass, wealthy bed
and you blush, eyeing
the leather muzzle
handcuffed to its head.
Like TV fuzz, the rain
comes in; your silk flowers
tremble in the wet, young air.
The nail polish burgeons
and the blender sings:
This obstinance called mud,
your mastering of spring.

MY MAN CALIBAN!

Were you (I suppose) expecting
an angry, homeboy soliloquy,
deep, gruff voice, spit cornering
some nigga mouth, a staccato repartee
replete with *muthafuckas, damn straights,*
and you (of course) could liberally recoil,
gape at those thick, angry lips,
mythologize my passion,
make sure you got first rights
to the movie version?

Well, I shan't… and you won't.
I mean, I really was going to lie
out in the sun on a slab
of concrete, legs thrown apart,
my manhood dangling and shit-
stupid angry, just waiting for
an Amber, a Kristin, a Helga,
you know: the black goat goes
for the does with hungry tongue.

But for some reason spring came
today, and that gash on my head
from that pop bottle you threw
is sprouting roses (you thought
was a scab). And that was you
on the steps of the teatro del negre
talkin' 'bout my momma and how
we all got tails, wasn't it?
Well, that's o.k. — I'll fix you some
punch spiked with collard green juice,
and that escargot you liked —
them's chitlins! Now, look at you:
greasy-mouthed, head throwed back,
grinning, belching, farting:
Caliban, my man!

A FIRST LADY CHALLENGES A LOA-AS-POEM

NEW YORK, Feb. 3, 2003 - "While Mrs. Bush respects the right of all Americans to express their opinions, she, too, has opinions and believes it would be inappropriate to turn a literary event into a political forum," Noelia Rodriguez, a spokeswoman for the first lady, said Wednesday.

I won't be in the same room with this poem.
And any space that sanctuaries it
will find me heartless, anything but warm

and tender. I itch with this lyric's foam
frothed up by some diphthong that quasi-fits.
I won't be in the same room with this poem.

Remember: I risk failure with both form
and sound. Why does it aurally resist
a muse once heartless, anything but warm?

Splendor's your calling card; *that's* how you worm
your way, never to lyrically commit.
I won't be in the same room with this poem.

Distemper shakes these very paws that comb
through tragic heaps of what was once fine wit
now rendered heartless, anything but warm.

Pretender! Prom-queen primed, ready to join
Shakespeare in séance, fixing to — Oh shit:
No more — not in the same room with a poem
where *Will* finds me heartless, anything but warm!

Tim Seibles, photograph by Lynda Koolish

Tim Seibles

4AM

I caught the last of a great caravan of clouds.
City night. Sky like the inside of a skillet

and, bright as ghosts, they crossed — not slowly
but unhurried — as if remembering the way

by feel, the way you might touch the wall
of a dark hall at a friend's house late, moving

toward the back porch where you heard the June-bugs
unbuttoning their brass jackets. September.

September: another good summer gone and me
another season older with these streets wet

from a small storm that woke me
to see silver clouds drawn along the sky,

but before that I had been dreaming: a box
of bottles on the back seat of a car, sunlight

steaming the windshield. A woman
wearing the bluest baseball cap

I ever saw. I guess I had been
driving, and somehow money

was involved, but neither of us knew
how much. We knew the police

were hiding in the church. "But look
how it is — " she said, "the road,

I mean, and wide," and the wind stuttered
in the thickening weeds and the asphalt stirred

like a dark sheet under which someone
sleeping had turned over   and then, it *was*

a river, much wider than a road,
with the wind barely brushing the trees

the way you might touch the hair of someone
you loved once, stumbling into her

underneath the marquee after a movie. It was difficult
smiling the brief embrace, seeing her walk away,

because her walk was the reason you had tried
to meet her five Junes ago — her smiling

voice, the almost sleepy grace in her gait.
You remember being mad at yourself

for *wanting* again, knowing that, eventually
she would come and go with her kind hands —

which she did — like the good season of a late hour,
like a brightness learning the dark by feel,

the way a blind-folded boy looks
for his friends in the basement: their quiet

so thick that he begins to wonder
if they are gone completely

which, in fact, they are — having one
by one slipped out the back door

where, after muffling their giggles, they find
a sunset rubbing brass into their tan jackets

and decide to just go home
while he goes on   tracing the walls,

the dusty sofa, the smooth plank
of the ironing board, believing his hands

will come to know their hidden places
which are not really there at all.

FRIEND AND BELOVED

I hope that we will meet again
if we meet again
I hope

we will meet again
if we meet
again   There was so

much I didn't say
this time   I hope we
will meet again if we

meet again   Will day break
night again
when we meet again

I won't be this
afraid again
when we meet
again   Won't that

be something
if we meet again I will play
again

when we
meet again if you'll
meet again   I won't

sleep again if we meet again
I hope we meet again

Shouldn't we
meet again
if we meet again   What

could I say
if we met again   The water
would be sweet

again if we met
again   Won't the trees
be tall again if we climb again

Would it be
here again if we met
again
Maybe we could try
to meet again

Or is again
not like again
I swear

we will meet
again if we meet again
Don't you think we'll

meet again
when we meet
again   I hope we
can meet
again if we meet

again   Would you
know that we'd met
again if we

met again when
we meet again   Would again
seem like again
again   I hope
we will meet again

if we meet
again when we
meet again

I hope
we will meet again

DOUGLASS, A LAST LETTER

"Am I always to be a black man, the runaway slave, living within and without the strictures of a corrupt society?"

In 1830 I was twelve and already I felt like a rare beast
marked time in my head, one whose incessant growls

meant to drive me mad   unless I could open
my skull and unpen the sleepless thing. Truthfully, it was

as if some creature, cold and hungry, were imprisoned
in a room with two openings — both too small for escape —

beyond which a sunlit orchard shone warm and redolent
with every kind of fruit, the taste and feel of which

could only be regarded with agonizing wonder and thirst.

Playing with some white children in Baltimore,
I quickly understood my life was not to be like theirs,

that decisions had been made about skin and the kind
of life that could be lived by anyone born darkly clad.

Being half-white helped little; unless one considers the twist
of the knife in the wound a help. As I approached twenty,

I wasn't religious exactly, but I'd come to believe any God
that could author these circumstances   could not merely

sit "on high" while I walked about with the lash at my back
and my head bursting with the wrongs I'd witnessed *and*

the alternatives to them which were, in fact, within
human reach. Why do white people persist

in a system that turns them into something monstrous.
It is not unlike laying out a great feast and being

compelled to salt each bite with ground glass. Why?
Why when good conscience must be bled

and good ears made deaf to shrink the heart so —
and why had I landed in such a world? I imagined God

probably sympathized, but His procrastination
worried me. Such was the noise in my head

as I climbed the years. That I was not killed by the weight
of these ruminations — or murdered because of them — strikes me

daily as a near miracle. I wanted *freedom.* Even the sound
throbbed like a broken rib inside me.

But I didn't really understand what *being* free
would mean. I must admit that, in this way, freedom

must be like *love*: none can know its quickening beauty
without having suffered its embrace.

When I met Ottilie Assing, I was already married
to Anna Murray, the woman who made my escape

possible. How could I not think her an angel? How
could I not feel a perennial debt, no matter how

much love I gave? I guess sometimes I resented her
doting, her kindness that had a tinge of something

else — as if she were *entitled* to me,
which, in part, I suppose she was,

though I'd drawn my fill of being *anyone's* property.

Without her help, of course, I could have been
many more years in bondage. The nauseating horror

of that prospect may never be clear
to someone who has never worn the yoke,

but suppose today
people began to see you and treat you

like a dog. Though you stood and spoke like a man,
you were given scraps to eat and were obliged to fetch

endlessly — knowing that any discontent would bring
the back of a hand, the cutting snap of a cow-skin.

Imagine how long a single day of this would be —
a month, a year. Most of you would rather die

than know what I've known. When I met Ottilie,
I had never known such a woman, boasting both

a boiling mind and a bright comeliness. I had not
been long from slavery. I did not know my voice

would bring me into such company. Her whiteness.
The way she regarded me unshyly. Was it possible

to touch, to kiss this woman   and survive? Even
to think it seemed insane, but if I was free —

like other men — didn't that mean I should feel
without fear and enact my passions

like other men? Of course, I was married
to a good woman, and Miss Assing bore the color

worthy of my stingiest glance,
but being German and Jewish, she knew something

of my anguish, too. My heart needed both
to hold her   and to lock her out,

lest it appear that I'd forgotten who I was.
Did white men skulking between the big house

and those clapboard shacks forget who *they* were —
crying their pleasure in the sad arms of colored women?

I was almost torn in half with wanting her and wanting
to be a husband whose love for his wife could

not be muddied by anything white. I didn't know
freedom   held so many damning choices.

I never believed I wouldn't get it
right which I don't think I did exactly:

Anna resented me, my duplicity, my looking
down on her small interest in books.

Ottilie was confused by the ever-changing menu
of my desire for her company — friend? lover? ally?

White abolitionists, who publicly raged about slavery,
privately thought her sullied and me, a lucky nigger

with a silver tongue

who didn't respect the decorum
of their generous permissions. Even on the eve

of Emancipation, I knew Lincoln held no fierce love
for those who languished in chains. My resentments

had multiplied so complexly, that I don't know why
I didn't end up snarling in some cage, why

madness didn't slake its thirst
on the sweat of my frenzy.

I have worked my mind as hard as any field I plowed in Maryland.
Shouldn't love be *color-blind?* Can I be

much more than a *Negro* racist
if my heart is shut to someone because of the skin

to which they were born? People say wait
until society is ready, but then I must ask why is the world

always ready to harvest the bounty of every
human depravity, while the time for installing

proper sanity is forever just beyond the green hills
strewn with corpses? We make society

by our deeds; we improve our lot by living
improved lives. Society need but shape itself fluidly

in accordance with our best efforts,
rather than making its misguided customs

a stone wall against which we are bound to see
our shoulders and the fists of our progeny —

black *and* white — broken and bloodied.

Let us perhaps be overly kind, and let this
strange America be re-cast by too much

good reason. Only this
can build a life that will not oblige our children

to suffer the perpetual extension
of these cruel mistakes. I say this

as a man who, having lived a long time
degraded by men, finds himself intoxicated

still   by what freedom *could* mean.

If, at times, I have seemed lost in my own
unmapped country or acted as one possessed

by a reckless thing, I believe I intended to be helpful
and truthfully — given what I was given and given

the interplay of passion and predicament —
I don't think I could have done other than I did.

Reginald Shepherd, photograph by Lynda Koolish

REFRAIN

A state becomes statement, Petrarch
trips on a pile of laurel bones, severely damaged
except for two lines. The body absorbs
all kinds of things, a useless brilliant nothing
guarding the borders of witness
where the metaphors start, and the snow.
Petrarch doesn't dream of snow, except
in silver bowls with syrup
mixed into it, pomegranate or persimmon
chasing summer somewhere next to lost,
and then the brilliant birds
fly from his mouth, perhaps
just one, a bird of paradise with no
legs, no feet, a lifetime's inability to land.

Petrarch whispers leaves into my ear,
thinks "Boys smell nice," boys smell
like spring preserved in a December jar, open
the lid and it escapes me just now, haunts
the room all day: stains air, stains
nostrils, cedar-pressed seasons sweetbitter
somewhat like eros, like crushed laurel
leaves stain fingers. He loves me nowhere
but in words (another of the several things
which I refrain from mentioning), boys' names
on trees or boys named after trees:
fixing beauty in the wind, fixing hunger
in the eye, the *x* of it. (I miss the men
midnighting Lakeview streets.)
Wind only visible in what it touches

leads astray, disturbing to discard;
trees shed their way toward nakedness
leaf by leaf until the bough has been broken.
A spatter of small nameable wings
takes to the wind, takes care not to wake
Petrarch, who's dreaming rain's
refrain, *fall down, fall down,*
but he's already one with grass.
And then a hero comes along
with birds flying out of his mouth:
one of the old verbs might be true,
park paths of wind-polished pebbles
lead one astray, into the snow.

BOY, ALLEGORICALLY DEPLOYED

Kiss the past until it's bitter, his
unexplored expanse of skin; cold coinage
of brass nipples kisses his chest tender
to the abrading tongue. He is what snows
in "it is snowing," precipitating indecision
and a sea of wavering white fields. Sheer
stipulation, verb, the act of being carried
out: bird water where finches drown
of thirst, a glass of axioms, half-full. (See,
we have bodies, and smell like the sea.)
Occasionally anyone.
                                        Ghostly geology,
slag and charnel leaf, slate face
with eroding fossils, this is not

his body: a damaged would-be nobility
disturbs the surfaces of things, even dust
fails me. The most beautiful boy
thinks "beautiful" is too large
and vacant, ripped open emptiness
on the left margin of argument:
thinks he can't remember whether I
remember no one's there, what he calls
himself. Calls himself *I* at times, and lies
down in a field of broken leaves
and shattered grass.
                                        Himself
on his way to being blazon, eyes ears
lips tongue, full catalogue of cartilage
and muscle and the saline bags
light seeps through. Lies down
and he is Atlas, hands lacking
labels for the lands his hands
land on. We have loved something
and moved on, carnage of pink balls
and buttocks, the world when looked at
properly, a game of names and places
no one's seen. Caress cold breath
until it rains (we've spoken of
the rain already), drown the day.
Then you'll be music too.

ITINERARY

for Robert Philen

Certain names have been ruined forever,
friendships snapped like dry twigs
underfoot. Whole people disappear
like little sovereign nights and aren't
missed (another useless world wavers);
he and I walk deeper into afternoon,
into the gorge. The visible and invisible
gods decree decay and change
it into duff, humus, and loam, into magnolia's
giant flowers that precede the green
wax leaves. What is that rotting
in the creek, gray-furred
and food for flies? A bird is an animal
with an inside and an outside, the green-
and purple-headed grackles
speckle the walled-in creek
bed, glisten from flat stone to round stone
searching out what. The highway says *No history*
here, a doe dozes beside the asphalt, or else
it's dead. It's dead. They line up single file
to cross the road, the first one waits
until the next one crosses. Look left,
look right, look left. The poems about nature
grow dry and brittle, crumble
like leaf-litter, rotting shale; we drop them
as we pass. The hand has held its secrets
for so long, he takes birdsong
into himself, and a grape soda smell
only in late June, another plant I can't

pin down. His skin subdues the sun
if he remembers rain, forecasting
overcast. Then he lets his sunset pierce
the hemlocks, quick pebbles tumble down
the slope's field of visual happiness.
The pines are singing water and we go
home, leave behind the cast-off instances.

HOMERIC INTERIM

Distance is money just out of reach,
a kindness like rain-laden clouds
that never drops its coins. Epochs
of fossilized trees crawl rusting hillside
strata: they smell like somewhere else
I've never been, an Anatolia
just outside the mind. Geometries
of travel and desire (from here to want
and back again), the myths of pleasure
reinvent another ancient world: oiled boys
racing naked around the circular walls
of Troy to find out who will wear
the plaited wreath, parade painted circuits
of unburnt parapets waving
to the crowds. See, even night
adores him, dresses him in its moon
and apparition. The sheen of intention
is on him, translates his motions
into marble, alabaster. (Cassandra
wakes and says *There isn't going to be*
a Trojan war. Centuries of fossil speech

fill up the space that comes after
currently, years spent talking
to paper.) Man and moment
become one, his reliquary skin
makes white occur (by now
the sweat has faded from his garish
details). The things his hands become
act out interruption, history
is his story, held at bay. He wears time
on his body (wears it out), chases gods
from mountaintops until the myth-smoke
clears. His old world's blurred
and hard to read, misunderstanding
becomes a place: galley
run aground on shallow skin
the color of no event.

OBJECTS IN MIRROR ARE CLOSER THAN THEY APPEAR

World Trade Center, September 11, 2001

I stow this moment with all the other baggage
too heavy to be carried or left
behind. Roadside church sign says *The Lord*
is the Lord who made us the way we are us.
He scatters the remnants and collects
them at a later date (unspecified): sorts them
into neat piles. I have watched twin towers fall
a dozen times. An absence moves through
the wreckage while the light stays put; the rats

will have to find another home.
Song keeps repeating *I watched you suffer*
even after the song's turned off.

History picks her way in high heels
through the structural redundancy (still shimmering
with its recentness, its haze of airborne ash
and grit), compassion makes his way through the structured
inequality in blue serge suit to interview survivors of
the structural adjustment, the combined
and uneven development that bursts into flames
at half an hour intervals, implodes
in slow motion with a televisual sigh
(catches up with photogenic falling bodies).

Song wants to soothe the sidewalk misery
into grief, smooth the debris into a shroud.

Lamed truth hobbles into another dark
through crumpled girders and concrete, calibrating
ruin and song, ruining the song
for the sake of what was life: hands out these
glass splinters, mercies and atrocities
that can't be lulled into music,
the ignorance we call innocence.
They taste like burning (a violent antidote),
incapable of caring if it harmonizes, or
unwilling to succumb again.

Song won't shut up, keeps saying *Don't look*
down. Justice tries to listen for a low tapping sound.

SELF-PORTRAIT IN THE NEW WORLD ORDER

You're walking down the street alone,
absorbed in the anticipation of a lunchtime salad
with that crusty olive bread you like so much,
and suddenly you're marching in formation
in a crowd, it's called a regiment.
You seem to be a soldier this time, you learn
to be at war. You're never really in danger
because you know you can't die
in your dreams, but sometimes
you wonder who told you that and whether
they could be trusted. The sidewalk is split
and uneven because of the shrapnel
and the artillery shells; yesterday
you didn't know the definition of artillery,
but today you know how to use it, all kinds
of field ordnance. "Ordnance" is a word
you'd never heard before. Every time
there's so much to notice, so much
to remember and write down. Here's
a little notebook with rubbed-down corners
for your back pocket. It's the little things
that distinguish one war from another,
tonight your shoes are black standard issue
marching boots that lace half-way up
your calves, whereas the other night
you had no shoes, or the shoes you'd lost
were beige bedroom slippers whose plush
offered no protection from the slush and rain
you trudged through. The subway crash
distracted you from that, now
you're climbing over the wreckage

to the next sheltered position, air thick
with morning mist (you're shivering), smoke
and a haze of acrid dust, it burns your lungs.
You're clambering through accordioned
cars, where are those twisted rails
that won't carry any passengers taking you?

Evie Shockley, photograph by Lynda Koolish

Evie Shockley

— shall become as —

you put this pen
in my hand and you
take the pen from
my hand. the night
before the full moon

the moon seems
full. what is missing
is a dark hungry
sickle, the sliver
of shadow eating

us up inside. after
the mountains breathe
their mint-and-sorrow
green against the long
summer sky, they burst

into hot october
laughter, lighting
the horizon with citrus,
rust, and blood. you
put this knife in my

        hand. we pull. we
meet as oceans come
together, heaving
        against and clinging
across our salt watery

        boundary. we approach
endlessly like two rails
of one track, tied
        in a parallel that
promises our eyes to

        merge, someplace far
off in the distance. you
put this feather in my
        palm. my fingers
close around flight.

cause i'm from dixie too

i am southern hear me roar i am burning flags bearing crosses i
am scarlett and prissy like a piece of carmine velvet at christmas
don't know nothing bout birthin no rabies so don't come foamin
at my mouth i am miss dixie and a miss is as good as a guile i
am a daughter of the con-federacy come on dad don't you know
me here let me put on this hood and sheet do my eyes look more
familiar now surrounded by bleach i am southern damn it y'all keep
forgetting my birth was our wedding till death do us part i took the
gal out of tennessee but the south came back to me the north left
me cold though there's southern heat i could do without i.e. stick
to barbequing cows and pigs but i'll take a late summer and a fall so
long i land right back in piedmont eden hell it's hot i am southern
got this drawl that comes from s-wallowing final consonants cuss
words loose meaning gonna spew it all back at you sew it in ink
on the fabric of a myth of a land of cotton on page after rotten
page book away book away book away dixie-banned o swee-tea
honey sugar dumpling pie i'll swallow more so much sweet stuff my
magnolias will shoot out blossoms protruding raw cane this is my
legacy the freak will inherit the mirth aw aw aw mammy don't you
want me don't you want me home come on mammy i mean miss
anne i may be your ugly duckling now but those folk up north will
see me no more when i get to that swan-y shore

FROM THE LOST LETTERS OF FREDERICK DOUGLASS

June 5, 1892

Dear Daughter,
Can you be fifty-three this
month? I still look for you to peek around
my door as if you'd discovered a toy
you thought gone for good, ready at my smile
to run up and press your fist into my
broken palm. But your own girls have outgrown
such games, and I cannot pilfer back time
I spent pursuing Freedom. Fair to you,
to your brothers, your mother? Hardly.

But
what other choice did I have? What sham,
what shabby love could I offer you, so
long as Thomas Auld held the law over
my head? And when the personal threat was
ended, whose eyes could mine enter without
shame, if turning toward my wife and children
meant turning my back?

Your mother's eyes stare
out at me through yours, of late. You think I
didn't love her, that my quick remarriage
makes a Gertrude of me, a corseted
Hamlet of you. You're as wrong as you are
lucky. Had Anna Murray had your
education as a girl, my love for
her would have been as passionate as it
was grateful. But she died illiterate,

when I had risked my life to master language.
The pleasures of book and pen retain
the thrill of danger even now, and you
may understand why Ottilie Assing,
come into our house to translate me into
German, could command so many hours,
years, of my time — or, as you would likely
say, of your mother's time.

Forgive me,
Rosetta, for broaching such indelicate
subjects, but as my eldest child and
only living daughter, I want you to
feel certain that Helen became the new
Mrs. Douglass because of what we shared
in sheaves of my papers: let no one
persuade you I coveted her skin.
I am not proud of how I husbanded
your mother all those years, but marriage,
too, is a peculiar institution.
I could not have stayed so unequally yoked
so long, without a kind of Freedom in
it. Anna accepted this, and I don't
have to tell you that her lot was better
and she, happier, than if she'd squatted
with some other man in a mutual
ignorance.

Perhaps I will post, rather
than burn, this letter, this time. I've written it
so often, right down to these closing lines,
in which I beg you to be kinder, much
kinder, to your step-mother. You two are

of an age to be sisters, and of like
temperament — under other circumstances,
you might have found Friendship in each other.

With regards to your husband — I am, as
ever, your loving father —

Frederick Douglass

my last modernist poem, #2
(or, mugshot)

don't say cover-up. this man's not masked,
he's the essence of out. the bare facts:
he's stripped his hair of naps, denuded
his skin, chiseled away the fleshy

roundness of his face. his eyes remain
geometrically opposed to his
jaw. don't say cover-girl. no, he's a
harlequin without his diamond tear,

mascaraed moats like tar encircling
his skewed view. ask yourself: who are his
models? liz or diana, maybe.
maybe he's reviving caesar or

catullus, based on a bust, forced to
cast himself in blood, sweat, and marble.

Lorenzo Thomas, photograph by Lynda Koolish

Lorenzo Thomas

DOWNTOWN BOOM

There are no gospel singers
Anymore

On the corners
They held down for Jesus
Valets park cars
At restaurants for fancy people
On expense accts or dates

So many times
People come up to me
And say, Billy
Hey wait a minute
You not Billy!

You can see the new ballpark
Just past the Courthouse

But which way is redemption?

DISCOVERING AMERICA AGAIN

In memory of Tom Dent

The world we found was not something
To fall in love with
But there were people in it
Who watched us at our games

Who warned us early
African veneers and European valences
Could both be false and
Polished surfaces distracting

Armed us with corny maxims
Pride is not assumed but earned
By effort properly applied

Common sense:
Garvey, Washington, Du Bois were men
Like those you meet in the street

And sent us on the way, expecting us
To be explorers
Space travelers in song,
Screaming or mellow
In caravans of ageless aspiration
To memorize exuberant manifests
Of semi-precious words

Discovering America again,
We found
The simplest of all mysteries
Called speech
Retains the register
Of fear

Encountering
What we do not know we know
Disguised as other people.

They are still there, those watchers
Watching you
Discovering America again

Don't be afraid —

Someone has walked this way before
All the world's music in her hands
Under the starlight
That she wished
Could lead away to freedom
Or at least a space to be
As newborn as tomorrow,
Forgiven as today

Someone has walked this way before
Who learned the secret

Someone has walked this way before:
A man who knew
That speech
Is breath made lovely
Shaped and shaping
Volume expanding both
Inside and out
In the quick transfer
Of sight and feeling
Into sound
            and sense (sometimes)

Someone has walked this way before,
My friend
Who was my friend

A man who spoke with people
Who asked you questions
So that you could breathe

SOUVENIR OF THE MANASSAH BALL

In truth,
Cordelia was a scorpion in blue
She called her divorce
"Independence Day"
You could hear the bombs bursting in air
She marched out like a majorette
And kicked her heels and cut her hair

"Pantomime Quiz" became the rage
At every party.
We danced around each slight and frown
A thousand brazen pairs of us
Rang in the city's chandeliers

We stung her way out of society
Then out of town

We found a charming cottage
In a nice suburb of Hell
Our tryst brought misspelled death threats
To her door:
A Barbie doll hung in a shoelace noose
A 10d nail driven between its legs.

But passion shields its servants from all harm
And her ex's wages kept the cottage warm

So, having stole the bride
Too late I knew
A misdirected Lochinvar
It's hard to assign victimhood
Or know who conquered who

She tied my ties
                    and combed my hair
I cooked for her
                    and read her books

Sometimes I was her splendid toy,
Sometimes her sword

And every moment thrilled our flesh with madness!

Natasha Trethewey, photograph by Lynda Koolish

BELLOCQ'S OPHELIA

from a photograph, circa 1912

In Millais's painting, Ophelia dies faceup,
eyes and mouth open as if caught in the gasp
of her last word or breath, flowers and reeds
growing out of the pond, floating on the surface
around her. The young woman who posed
lay in a bath for hours, shivering,
catching cold, perhaps imagining fish
tangling in her hair or nibbling a dark mole
raised upon her white skin. Ophelia's final gaze
aims skyward, her palms curling open
as if she's just said, *Take me.*

I think of her when I see Bellocq's photograph —
a woman posed on a wicker divan, her hair
spilling over. Around her, flowers —
on a pillow, on a thick carpet. Even
the ravages of this old photograph
bloom like water lilies across her thigh.
How long did she hold there, this other
Ophelia, nameless inmate in Storyville,
naked, her nipples offered up hard with cold?

The small mound of her belly, the pale hair
of her pubis — these things — her body
there for the taking. But in her face, a dare.
Staring into the camera, she seems to pull
all movement from her slender limbs

and hold it in her heavy-lidded eyes.
Her body limp as dead Ophelia's,
her lips poised to open, to speak.

Note: Ophelia is the imagined name of a prostitute photographed circa 1912 by E. J. Bellocq, later collected in the book, Storyville Portraits. A very white-skinned black woman — mulatto, quadroon, or octoroon — she would have lived in one of the few "colored" brothels such as Willie Piazza's Basin Street Mansion or Lula White's Mahogany Hall, which, according to the Blue Book, was known as the "Octoroon Club."

LETTER HOME

New Orleans, November 1910

Four weeks have passed since I left, and still
I must write to you of no work. I've worn down
the soles and walked through the tightness
of my new shoes, calling upon the merchants,
their offices bustling. All the while I kept thinking
my plain English and good writing would secure
for me some modest position. Though I dress each day
in my best, hands covered with lace gloves
you crocheted — no one needs a *girl*. How flat
the word sounds, and heavy. My purse thins.
I spend foolishly to make an appearance of quiet
industry, to mask the desperation that tightens
my throat. I sit watching —

though I pretend not to notice — the dark maids
ambling by with their white charges. Do I deceive
anyone? Were they to see my hands, brown
as your dear face, they'd know I'm not quite
what I pretend to be. I walk these streets
a white woman, or so I think, until I catch the eyes
of some stranger upon me, and I must lower mine,
a *negress* again. There are enough things here
to remind me who I am. Mules lumbering through
the crowded streets send me into reverie, their footfall
the sound of a pointer and chalk hitting the blackboard
at school, only louder. Then there are women, clicking
their tongues in conversation, carrying their loads
on their heads. Their husky voices, the wash pots
and irons of the laundresses call to me. Here,

I thought not to do the work I once did, back-bending
and domestic; my schooling a gift — even those half days
at picking time, listening to Miss J — . How
I'd come to know words, the recitations I practiced
to sound like her, lilting, my sentences curling up
or trailing off at the ends. I read my books until
I nearly broke their spines, and in the cotton field,
I repeated whole sections I'd learned by heart,
spelling each word in my head to make a picture
I could see, as well as a weight I could feel
in my mouth. So now, even as I write this
and think of you at home, *Good-bye*

is the waving map of your palm, is
a stone on my tongue.

from "STORYVILLE DIARY"

(Self) Portrait

On the crowded street I want to stop
time, hold it captive in my dark chamber —
a train's sluggish pull out of the station,
passengers waving though open windows,
the dull faces of those left on the platform.
Once, I boarded a train; leaving my home,
I watched the red sky, the low sun glowing —
an ember I could blow into flame — night
falling and my past darkening behind me.
Now I wait for a departure, the whistle's
shrill calling. The first time I tried this shot
I thought of my mother shrinking against
the horizon — so distracted, I looked into
a capped lens, saw only my own clear eye.

VIGNETTE

from a photograph by E. J. Bellocq, circa 1912

They pose the portrait outside
the brothel — Bellocq's black scrim,
a chair for her to sit on. She wears
white, a rhinestone choker, fur,
her dark crown of hair — an elegant image,
one she might send to her mother.
Perhaps the others crowd in behind

Bellocq, awaiting their turns, tremors
of laughter in their white throats.
Maybe Bellocq chats, just a little,
to put her at ease while he waits
for the right moment, a look on her face
to keep in a gilded frame, the ornate box
he'll put her in. Suppose he tells her
about a circus coming to town — monkeys
and organ music, the high trapeze — but then

she's no longer listening; she's forgotten
he's there. Instead she must be thinking
of her childhood wonder at seeing
the contortionist in a sideshow — how
he could make himself small, fit
into cramped spaces, his lungs
barely expanding with each tiny breath.
She thinks of her own shallow breath —
her back straining the stays of a bustier,
the weight of a body pressing her down.
Picture her face now as she realizes
that it must have been harder every year,
that the contortionist, too, must have ached
each night in his tent. This is how
Bellocq takes her, her brow furrowed
as she looks out to the left, past all of them.
Imagine her a moment later — after
the flash, blinded — stepping out
of the frame, wide-eyed, into her life.

Anthony Walton, photograph by Elizabeth Stern

Anthony Walton

DISSIDENCE

in memoriam Thelonious Monk

You have to be able to hear past the pain, the obvious
minor-thirds and major-sevenths, the merely beautiful

ninths; you have to grow deaf to what you imagine
are the sounds of loneliness; you have to learn indifference

to static, and welcome noise like rain, acclimate
to another kind of silence; you have to be able to sleep

in the city, taxis and trucks careening through your dreams
and back again, hearing the whines and sirens and shrieks

as music; you must be a mathematician, a magician
of algebra, overtone and acoustics, mapping the splintered

intervals of time, tempo, harmony, stalking or sluicing blues
scales; you have to be unafraid of redundance, and aware

that dissonance-driven explorations of dissonance
may circle back to the crowded room of resolution;

you have to disagree with everything except the piano, black
and white keys marking the path you must climb step

by half-step with no compass but the blues, no company
but your distrust of the journey, of all that you hear, of arrival.

GWENDOLYN BROOKS

Sometimes I see in my mind's eye a four or five
year old boy, coatless and wandering
a windblown and vacant lot or street
on the windblown South Side. He disappears
but stays with me, staring and pronouncing
me guilty of an indifference more callous
than neglect, condescension as self-pity.

Then I see him again, at ten or fifteen, on the corner,
say, 47th and Martin Luther King, or in a group
of men surrounding a burning barrel off Lawndale,
everything surrounding vacant or for sale.
Sometimes I trace him on the train to Joliet
or Menard, such towns quickly becoming native
ground to these boys who seem to be nobody's
sons, these boys who are so hard to love, so hard
to see, except as case studies.

Poverty, pain, shame, one and a half million
dreams deemed fit only for the most internal
of exiles. That four-year-old wandering
the wind tunnels of Robert Taylor, of Cabrini
Green, wind chill of an as yet unplumbed degree —
a young boy she did not have to know to love.

THE ENCYCLOPEDIA OF RHYTHM AND BLUES

Passion killings, plane crashes, overdoses,
accidental and intended;

Suicides, bus wrecks, women;
the inability to choose between one

woman and another; heroin, booze, the inability
to choose between pleasure

and the Lord; men, prison, the white man,
the white man who owns

the record company; all of this delineated
as melismatic celebration

of disaster and the gut-wrenching agony
of joy, the anger and hush of the naked

soul alone, sighing and shouting intensely
hyperbolic declarations of erotic

heroism — *anywhere, baby, anyhow,*
skidding out of control and into the next-

to-the-last chorus and over the bridge and key
change, popping the balloon of a heart inflated

with humiliation and pain and replacing it
with guttural and shrieking glissandos

— I once was lost and now am found —
as if a singer were an angel commissioned

in the highest holy orders, as if a song had wings
extended into flight and feathers of shelter —

as if true love and its fraternal twin, the blues,
possessed equally the powers of devotion

and redemption, as if the one true heaven
were standing around the corner, laughing

drunk, and locked with lust and abandon
into the everloving arms of the mortal world.

MCDONALD'S, SCOTTSBORO, APRIL, 1997

The white girl smiles
and hands me
my meal, perfectly
happy, it seems,
to see me, a black

man smiling
and accepting
a warmed-over
quarter-pound of meat
with cheese.

I am on the road,
rolling through
Jackson County,
here for food and gas
on my way
to Tennessee.

The way her pink
and silver-ringed
fingers touch mine —
so benign, as if time
and the town were
as innocent as she.

What is this to me,
who needs to eat
and keep moving,
to be in Tennessee
by midnight? I resolve
to leave history

behind me, resuming
my journey, the ride
up U.S. 72 into
and through Jackson
County, into what I fear
and only remember,
and only remember here.

ELEGY FOR JOAN
(1955-1986)

You did not bend
or break,
but simply sailed
away.

I could only chase as your heavy blossom snapped
and snagged the wind,
over waves of grass, trees, flowers...

Too soon. The epistle of my grief lengthens
each night, I revise
but cannot send.

I can spend my days anywhere, Times Square,
in a field of faces
                    running for the rain
or back in Illinois considering
a field of infinite blue cornflowers,
but having outlived your death, I can't outlive
you. Time passes,
                    but what is time
except the never-ending present punctuated
by what it takes away?

You knew you were dying,
and you did
                    with an equanimity so full of peace
it bordered on rage, which is where
I live,
                    and owe you goodbye.

Not this mooning through cities,
through blue fields holding your face
like a flower before me, my blossom
in bloom,
                        already doomed.

Crystal Williams, photograph by Owen Carey

Crystal Williams

HAPPINESS

Now, it's true that Happiness was a little cockeyed & her dress was a particular yellow & when she laughed she sounded, well, something akin to a donkey. But, our boy Ollie was not a little bit thick. I mean, when he was young he cried & yelped even when he'd been given all the Legos. &, it wasn't that he had turned into a stupid man. Or even a blind man. He was just, well, stubborn. So, they stood in the park like that for some time, oblivious to everything; folks milled around. At one point, someone's kid stuck his head under Happiness's dress until his mother yanked him out. The point is, Happiness & her cockeyed self & Ollie & his thick headed self were standing off. Happiness whose parents, Patience & Gratitude, had taught her well kept saying, "but I am here, you've been calling & I've come." & Ollie kept saying, "But you're cockeyed & I don't want cockeyed happiness." "Well," she'd huff, "I'm what you've got." They went round & round like that. Meanwhile, Patience, whose friends mostly called him Pat because his given name sounded feminine & he wasn't a feminine sort, went to the park to see what had kept his daughter away. He found her next to the teeter-totter in that really odd yellow dress, staring down some fool of a man who himself was no Adonis. Pat sat on the bench for an hour before pulling a crying Happiness away. After she'd gone Ollie stood there for some time feeling not quiet right. Children ran around him, a dog used his leg. & at 8:05 post meridian, our boy Ollie realized it was cold & dragged his sorry butt home. You know the rest. He ate, he shat & took some months to figure out any Happiness is better than none.

RITUAL

These Vietnamese women might as well be Jesus & we with our crusty,
boiled feet, his disciples. Old, this ritual. Water, hand & foot. Here
in Vogue Nails hunched in humility they wash, scrub & polish our feet.

When Miss Thing walks in we all glance up & then ogle entranced.
She is exquisite, a mix of men, dark & light, maybe persian
or some domestic blend. I don't imagine that it matters

to the young girl in the middle chair who this morning tried her very best:
her whitest bustier, her dear pink scalloped skirt.
& for a moment she was lovely. Here now, her face is full-on torrent:

astonished
& then bewildered
& then anger settles in a sour glower.

Swift is the moment of death & birth:
the young woman oblivious to the world
the new woman beginning to grasp the edges of it. & I am sad

that this regular girl now knows she is regular,
understands something of what will never be.
I want to go over & say something, but it is a private moment

& there is nothing here but great loss: the husky quiet of the forest trees,
the moment the world rustles unevenly & you know nothing of it
& you understand nothing but that you cannot change it.

ON FORGETTING YOUR FATHER'S FACE

for mel, after eddie

Girl, it is slow, the forgetting of a face.
This is how it goes: the edges blur,
flesh & blood pull & yawn away from their carcass.
& one day: gone.
& you'll think yourself an awful daughter
because surely a father's face should remain sharp as first light.
So, like all of us who are without,
you will rummage through the boxes of your mind, searching
& finding nothing but books, each holding another truth,
a bigger, more succulent lesson. But you won't want lessons. So, you'll continue
to unpack & unpack until nothing makes sense,
until the stories of your life whirl & clamor & whirl & whirl
& all the while your heart like all hearts will moan
& lament its circumstance. But, the heart is a beautiful monster,
it near always survives its fate.
Believe me when I say it is not a picture you seek.   Someday
in a long while when you have given in
to failed memory, to the lost pictures of your father,
when you are out of grief & your girl body relaxes finally into womanhood,
someone will ask a question for which you should have no answer
& you will answer & the soft tissue of your body for that second
will look leaner, more male & for a moment, gloriously,
beyond you.

NEGRO SURVIVAL 101 OR POEM FOR TIGER WOODS AND OTHER MULTIETHNIC *OTHER'S*

The math is as old as Medusa's left tit. Boy,
Fuzzy, that joker, don't want no collards & fried chicken
at next year's meet. Of course, you weren't supposed to be
offended.   Little Brother,
total your parts however you like.
No matter how hard & wide you swing that stick,
first lesson in Negro Survival 101 will always be this:
'Round these parts, Math don't mean shit —
even Fuzzy knows that.'

SUGAR

Girl, when his tongue is all sugar, suddenly
sweetened on the way u walk, dress,
be careful; when he begins to see u as candy,
something to be sucked on & swallowed,
look to his feet. Is he walkin' u're way
or are his dogs tucked beneath him?
That carpet is all magic & mirrors,
Babydoll. In the beginning was the word
but then there wuz feet: be wary of the pigeon-toed fool
barely steppin & offerin too much sugar for a nickel.

SHOP SONNET

for willie

saturday mornings in harlem at places
where black is still beautiful & press-n-curls still in,
Man comes with lips full of our names & eyes bright
as the rhinestone jammies I'm gluing to Girl's nails.
Dollar-man. Local — it's all deodorant & nivea, batteries.
Federal — some trucker-who-ain't-never-been-'round-here's
load: clothes & shoes & shit to primp. Don't ask
no question, you ain't gettin' no lie. We stop.
Shop girls, nail girls, do my hair girls, hop & bop
to Man's news. Laugh, gasp: the lock down, beat
down, the *damn Tyrell got gone down.*
When it all gets broke down we put our numbers
on a cloud, send Man on his way. Pay the nickel,
though it'll cost a dime.

Tyrone Williams, photograph by Lynda Koolish

Tyrone Williams

ASK-VUBBA: A DECALOGUE

for Steve McCaffery

"So We Are Told To Write Down"

The brain throws [out] its voice —

"errors" on the mind

Ballpark figures plump when you cook 'em

I do in fact care for

I am repeatedly acoustically wound

You come through — then "in"

And the blur draws us out, in, through

Allure as our only

{Leftovers experience difficulty — are not

presently available)

Plan B — Walk, Listen

Because everyone is outside, has been accounted for, the auto-garbled cave shrinks into a scrawled-over cast.

An ear infection degrades triangulation features, so I cannot tell if the banging on the basement door is coming from "above" or "below." There are no sidewalks outside the strip mall, for these words, often misunderstood, have no lifestyle other than the shape of traffic, of commerce, subsumed under transcendental zoning laws.

If lose my balance and so my place in line, will you hear "that"? The phone is ringing — are you going to get "it"?

There
I
Is

Planet X

You do —
or can —
or will —
not repeat my selves.

I told myself
(Did not get It).

Did so.

Did well
And then

Didn't.

Planned Community

NAACP

[cccp]

NCAA

A chance to sit at the big tax table.

A golfbag of irons and emery boards.

NOW

[did too]

Other Wards Of The Hospice

from the get-go
back

Number name normative. Outflanked

opposable capitals
retool oneself

"Everything hinges..."
on the necessity of

quotation marks.

* * *

In a fireplace the flames gasp for greener
campfires

No declasse rent but all utilities paid for by the land
_99

Enjambment disables the following with affective
minimals

Xenophobic idioms blame miscarriages on labor collapses
back into

lower work
Standards at an angle=another angle spun-spelled angel

Brief

Dainty feet

(padded shoulders)

slip into

(sofa throws)*

a pair of mules

(cake-let)

*See also wraps, stoles, etc.

Closing (as)

Dogs don't suffer from insomnia even when they cannot sleep, so this bark "is melting in the dark/all [its] sweet green icing flowing down," a numinous bark asea seeking <u>nommo</u>, this bark variously dubbed Kon-Tiki, Ra, Ra II, Tigris, this bark which "might have had more fun" as a mere ring among rings (awaiting its own pick-up operator), this bark which might have grown a pair of oars, bites.

Ditto (at)

Prone to be a (s)he-man with pillow underhead means blue chip. Place the pillow overface and the portfolio soars through the skylight. As for the head merely among, simply between, only beside, a pillow, one can only ensure the throw of a die, the other held back, in reserve, until the gambit tumbles to a stop.

P.P.S. (am)

We were always going to move to the city of recommended summer readings. That was the story of a self-made you this. Supposed, we shuttle back and forth as do this, don't do that. Here ends there, the voiceover lags.

To To Speak

The concave dish of reason for a few waves
convoluted, licentious ears. Eecchhooeess

from now. A hand-set type. Letters rise up
against the word but remain embedded in their plates

of relative license (cf. Freedmen's Bureau): collagen,
silicone and lipowhite: Resolution 1195: "a leader

in the quest for civil rights and justice"
[scale and base invariant]. A see-and-feel-

through Voice
for Good.

Herman Beavers

THE ARCHIVAL IMPULSE IN AFRICAN AMERICAN POETRY: PLAYING IN THE PAST

1

In his excellent volume, *Silencing the Past: Power and the Production of History,* anthropologist Michel-Rolph Trouillot asserts that the social process we understand as history "involves peoples in three distinct capacities: 1) as *agents*, or occupants of structural positions; 2) as *actors* in constant interface with a context; and 3) as *subjects*, that is, as voices aware of their vocality."[1] Trouillot's formulation is equally useful in attempting to understand the recent turn in contemporary African American poetry, particularly in the works of younger poets, toward a rumination on historiography and, by implication then, history. African American poets seeking both to understand their own place in history and how history may be working inside them are likewise a way to reproduce Trouillot's "three distinct capacities."

But I wish to place Trouillot's argument alongside Theodore O. Mason's observation regarding the *Norton Anthology of African American Literature*, that such a moment in literary history "provides an index to African American literature's postcolonial status." Citing Benedict Anderson's *Imagined Communities*, Mason characterizes the *Norton Anthology* as an instance where such a postcolonial

> moment marks the need for a remapping, a retaking of the census, a reorganization of the museum, not with an eye toward the good of the colonial power, but rather toward the good of the previously colonized, now emerging into nationhood. In fact, such a moment is deeply involved in the reconstruction, not the eradication, of difference, something absolutely connected with the idea of a literature anthology. (191)

Taken together, Trouillot's and Mason's respective observations help both to frame and to situate the project at hand. For in undertaking

[1] Michel-Rolph Trouillot. *Silencing the Past: Power and Production of History.* (Boston: Beacon Press, 1995). p. 23.

to produce an anthology whose purpose is mapping the "Diversity in African American Poetry," the contributors to the volume are working, perhaps consciously, toward a potentially path-breaking inquiry. By using the word "diversity" in the title of the conference, the organizers denotated an important area of struggle, one possessing the potential either to change the way American poetry is conceptualized or leave it mired in the same stock notions of diversity one finds in corporate culture. There, we find calls for the need to "manage diversity" which suggests that while numbers of the underrepresented and excluded may increase, power will remain firmly in the hands of the dominant group. In looking at a range of poetry anthologies, dating back to *Naked Poetry* (1969), edited by Stephen Berg and Robert Mezey and *Black Fire* (1968), edited by Amiri Baraka and Larry Neal, up through more recent anthologies ranging from Dave Smith and David Bottoms's influential *Morrow Anthology of Younger American Poets* (1985) to Kevin Powell and Ras Baraka's *In the Tradition: An Anthology of Young Black Writers* (1992), it is clear that anthological practices in the United States reflect a profound level of racial and cultural polarization.[2]

Though it would be inaccurate to suggest that the kind of racial animus exemplified by, say, Wallace Stevens towards Gwendolyn Brooks on the occasion of his service on the selection committee for the 1952 National Book Award,[3] constitutes a consensus of any consequence in

[2] We would do well to remember Richard Merelman's notion of cultural projection, where he posits four distinct forms: syncretism, hegemony, polarization, and counter-hegemony (5). For our purposes here, anthologies produced since the late 60s have approached inclusiveness in ways that reflect either a syncretic or polarized ethos. Which is to say that the anthologies mentioned above were intended to serve either a taxonomic function or a corrective one. In the former instance, the anthology captures all that is worthy of display as a way to suggest that which (or those whom) a qualified judge would be led to include (or exclude) in the matter of constituting a "national literature." In the latter, various groups attempt to "correct" the genealogical record of a national literature by positing its own list of worthy subjects. At some level, the tension between the two approaches has the potential for "covering the bases," but I am concerned, nonetheless, that either approach runs the risk of masking its politics behind the rhetoric of expediency. See Merelman, *Representing Black Culture: Racial Conflict and Cultural Politics in the United States.* (New York: Routledge, 1995), Chaps. 1-6.

[3] Rachel Blau DuPlessis, in an essay entitled, "Darken Your Speech: Racialized Cultural Work of Modernist Poets," makes note of Stevens's behavior as a way to suggest what she describes as his "unarguable racial prejudices," in contradistinction to the work of his biographer, Joan Richardson, who insists that Stevens identifies with blackness, much in the way of Whitman, in several of his poems written in the 1930s and observes apologetically that Stevens's racial "ambivalences" were "due to the circles in which he moved." DuPlessis's work here carries out elements of the project begun by Toni Morrison in her book *Playing in the Dark*. It is one of several fine efforts to be found in Aldon Lynn Nielsen's fine collection of essays, *Reading Race in American Poetry* (Urbana, IL: University of Illinois Press, 2000), pp. 43-83.

American poetry, it would also be a distortion to suggest that acts of inclusion have been either swift or decisive. What this suggests, at the risk of taking the road much traveled, is that another approach to the matter of diversity is required. Certainly, it is difficult to object to the idea that African American poets can be situated along an unusually broad spectrum of aesthetic styles, ideologies, and regional origins. And if one goes a few steps further and considers the impact on the poet's medium of language, it quickly becomes clear that diversity is perhaps best thought of as verb rather than as noun.

2

In order to pursue the notion of diversity as verb, I have selected five poets from the anthology: Honorée Fanonne Jeffers, Timothy Seibles, Evie Shockley, Anthony Walton, and Natasha Trethewey. The selection is based as much on the ways their respective approaches to history depart from one another as they approximate each other. Moving through each poet's respective poems, in some instances singular poems, in others a series of poems, it becomes clear that these poets have in most instances eschewed the topicality of the Black Arts Movement in favor of a slightly different relationship to the past. Unlike Morrison's Sethe, whose life becomes consumed with the effort of "holding the past at bay," these poets often demonstrate the ways that history can burst past its boundaries, influencing, if not altering, the ways we navigate the present. For example, in Honorée Fanonne Jeffers's powerful "Tuscaloosa: Riversong," she relates the story of the fateful encounter in Southern Alabama between the warrior-chief, Tuscaloosa, and the Spanish conqueror, Hernando DeSoto. In a manner that reflects Trouillot's three distinctions, Jeffers assumes at various points in the poem, the role of subject, actor, and agent. In Part I, "Black Warrior Speaks," Tuscaloosa notes DeSoto's arrival and declares, "We are strong against these whites / with sticks like dirty breath, / these silly children snatching toys." By opening the poem in this way, Jeffers puts forward a vision of history that is alternately cosmological and eschatological. Moreover, we note the way that

Tuscaloosa begins "The night before they came, / I walked on my river." Such a declaration not only recalls Christ's miraculous act, it exemplifies a similar intensity of faith. However, it also intimates the manner in which Christianity will supplant, if it does not destroy it outright, the Indian's religious beliefs.

But perhaps most useful for our purposes is the way Part I ends, for there, Tuscaloosa asserts that when "walking on [his] river" he is invisible. His realization that the Spanish "choke on [the] songs" of his people proposes that if 'speaking is translating' then the Spanish conquistadores' inability or unwillingness to learn his language likewise suggests the ways they fail to see Tuscaloosa and his kind as historical subjects — a more serious crime, since DeSoto's construction of the indigenous people of Florida, Alabama, and Louisiana comes to be the template for how other Europeans will understand them. This is confirmed by Part 2 of the poem, "DeSoto speaks." For there, DeSoto speaks in anger at Tuscaloosa's determination to defeat him. In DeSoto's view, the Indians have committed the even greater transgression of insisting that their religiosity is powerful enough to withstand the Spanish expansionist project. The extent to which DeSoto takes offense at Tuscaloosa's resistance is evidenced by his statement, "I want his mouth / wounded with slime." We come to understand this as a desire that assumes both figurative and literal shape. Tuscaloosa is killed, his people pushed off a bluff into the river below, where they drown by the thousands. The warrior-chief's "mouth / wounded with slime," also suggests DeSoto's rejection of the voice of the Indian, his declaration that translation is unnecessary. It is equally suggestive of the ways that the Indian voice will be archived in history, with the river becoming the repository where it will be kept hidden until someone, like Jeffers, comes along to release that voice. Hence, Jeffers ends the poem by assuming the responsibility of calling out to Tuscaloosa's spirit, thereby communing with him. The poem's concluding lines, "do not walk across my river / do this in remembrance of me," not only come to us in the voice of Tuscaloosa, but they also propose that at those moments when past transgressions are redressed, ancestry has its widest possible meaning; one does not have to be an Indian to be a witness. In this instance, walking "across the water," not only refers to what it means for rivers to be bridged by human labor, but also to the more historically resonant matter at hand: acts of remuneration are invalidated if one repeats the original transgression. In calling for prayer in Part 5, Jeffers has already recognized that such an act makes her one of Tuscaloosa's kin. Inevitably, the poem is suggestive of the ways that it is geography, here, in the form of the river, that, as Ralph Ellison insisted, determines fate, not only of a personal sort, but on a national scale as well.

But we could juxtapose Jeffers's poem, which presents history through a shifting perspectivity, against Walton's "McDonald's, Scottsboro, April, 1997." While the speaker's position in time and space is established by the poem's title, the reader is nonetheless led through a brief encounter in a fast-food restaurant that constitutes the speaker's fall into the historical abyss of the Scottsboro Boys trial. The courtesy shown him by the young white girl behind the counter, her smiling innocence, the way her hand touches his in a manner described as "benign," all combine to collapse the temporal and spatial barriers between March, 1931 and April, 1997. Which is to say that Walton's poem becomes a way for the reader to ruminate upon the lasting effects of accumulated sin.

Indeed, for the poem's speaker, the white girl's efforts to serve him ultimately call attention both to racial progress and its cost. The price, we discover, is exacted in the form of remembering the past, of being forced to remember the ways that human bodies in a place so synonymous with injustice and racial humiliation are indelibly stained by the intersection of geography and history. And though his time in Scottsboro, Alabama is due to be brief, the simple act of having a meal in McDonald's, rather than becoming the representation of the speaker's mobility and status (as intimated by his smiling face and the fact that Scottsboro is a stop but not a destination) is revealed for what it is. The "quarter-pound of meat / with cheese" is by no means adequate reparation. And thus, to be a black man "smiling /

and accepting" such a worthless prize casts the speaker into a state of historical flux, a state of exigency so insistent that the banality of the act forces him to remember that it was an alleged act of interracial physical contact — here, the insistence by Ruby Bates and Victoria Price that they were raped by nine black boys on a train — that has made this town infamous.

The speaker concludes to "keep moving, / to be in Tennessee / by midnight," an effort that will require him to "leave history // behind" But his journey can only be completed by realizing that the journey is now "into" not "away from." As such, we can read the poem's final two lines as the act of giving voice to what history demands of the speaker, but it also can be read, as the visual referent for what is demanded of the reader. Thus, "and only remember, / and only remember here," is an instance of homonymic play, for "here" can also be "hear," marking Walton's use of an African American vernacular formation, where the word "hear" is a command whose aim is to target that place where aurality and obedience become synonymous.

But if the aforementioned poets attempt to postulate the vagaries of difference on a racial grid, there is also no shortage of poems in the anthology that attempt to account for gender difference as well. This could be the reason that the issues of voice — and voicing — that inhere in poetry lend themselves well to a consideration of gender identity as it gets performed in African American poetry. For example, two poems in the anthology, Evie Shockley's "The Lost Letters of Frederick Douglass" and Tim Seibles, "Douglass, A Last Letter," are remarkable poems in their own right. What fascinates me here is that two poets, at two distinctly different points in their respective careers, working independently, not only select Frederick Douglass as poetic subject, but moreover, opt to convey Douglass's story in the epistolary form. This would be remarkable in and of itself, but when we read the poems and note that both poems are set in motion, moving toward a consideration of Douglass's courtship and subsequent marriage to his second wife, Helen, we must conclude that something much more significant is afoot.

Shockley's poem is framed as part of a corpus of Douglass's lost correspondence, with the poem we are reading rendered in the guise of a letter from an elderly Douglass to his middle-aged daughter, Rosetta. Dated June 5, 1892, the poem begins with Douglass's amazement that his daughter has reached the age of fifty-three. The first stanza ends with Douglass's assertion that he cannot "pilfer back time / I spent pursuing Freedom" and the appended comment that this incapacity was unfair to Rosetta, her brothers, and mother.

As a letter directed to his daughter, Douglass's intent becomes clear as a dual gesture of reconciliation and explanation. Hence, we need to pay close attention to the word "Lost" in the title, for through its use, Shockley suggests that this is a letter that was either never sent or if posted, deemed unworthy of historical mention. As one letter among many, Shockley's act of poetic composition is made noteworthy because she does not shrink from the difficult task of producing a poem that captures Douglass's expansive rhetorical style, even as it suggests that his desire to be understood, and perhaps forgiven, is a force so violent it can barely be contained.

Seibles's poem has a wider narrative sweep, opening with Douglass harkening back to his youth in the year 1830, when, he says, "I felt like a rare beast / marked time in my head, one whose incessant growls // meant to drive me mad unless I could open / my skull and unpen the sleepless thing." Douglass uses the "rare beast" as a way to metaphorize his desire for freedom. But, Seibles powerfully elaborates on this opening metaphor, transforming it from a rare beast intent on compromising his sanity to a "creature, cold and hungry ...imprisoned / in a room with two openings — both too small for escape — // beyond which a sunlit orchard shone warm and redolent/with every kind of fruit, the taste and feel of which // could only be regarded with agonizing wonder and thirst." In Seibles's rendering, Douglass moves from wanting to be shut of the beast growling in his skull, to empathizing with the beast's desire to be warm and fed.

In composing a "Last" letter for Douglass, Seibles's poem attempts to cover much of the territory addressed in Douglass's three autobiographies. With a difference, of course, for we quickly note the way Douglass's letter turns, not toward his second wife, but toward his friend and confidante (and, as Douglass biographer William McFeely surmises, lover), Ottilie Assing. "When I met Ottilie, / " Douglass's "letter" insists, "I had never known such a woman, boasting both // a boiling mind and a bright comeliness. I had not / been long from slavery. I did not know my voice // would bring me into such company." The formal differences between the two poems notwithstanding (Seibles's poem is longer and in couplets, Shockley's in a much more open form, with stanzas that run between 2 and 18 lines), what is striking — and exciting — about their shared presence in this volume is their mutual interest in Douglass's vexed marriage to his first wife, Anna.

We could most certainly conclude that both Shockley and Seibles are partaking of the numerous discussions surrounding interracial dating and marriage in the present moment, in effect, using a historical figure to grind polemical axes, but such a conclusion misses the point. What is distinctive here is the impulse to represent within the space of poetic — as opposed to novelistic — discourse the life of an African American historical figure, not to lionize him (as Robert Hayden does so ably in his sonnet, "Frederick Douglass"), but rather to complicate him. Though Douglass comes through in both poems as opportunistic and self-serving, both poems help us to understand the "historical figure" because they present him as *actor* in a context rather than as *subject* becoming aware of his vocality. The Douglass who comes to us in both poems is beyond this, though in Seibles' rendering, he recalls what his life was like prior to literacy.

Finally, I want to turn my attention to Natasha Trethewey's poems from the excellent *Bellocq's Ophelia*. In the three poems anthologized here, Trethewey establishes the personae of Ophelia and E.J. Bellocq as agents, seeking to accomplish ends that reflect their positions in New Orleans society in 1912. Though it would be easy to construe their relationship as exploitative, a manifestation of the racial and sexual domination institutionalized in the photographic image, Trethewey suggests once again that complexity demands a deeper interrogation.

It is not that race and gender are not important aspects of this drama, but Trethewey's attention is focused on the ways that the cultural imaginary invents vehicles to further its ends, a circumstance in which black women are often victimized.

Thus, in "Letter Home," we find Ophelia newly arrived in the city, seeking employment each day, wearing lace gloves to disguise her hands, dressed in her best clothes, hoping her "plain English and good writing" can "secure / …some modest position." We do not discover until the second stanza of the poem that she is passing for white. "I walk these streets / a white woman, or so I think, until I catch the eyes / of some stranger upon me, and I must lower mine, / a *negress* again." What becomes clear is that Ophelia, who will become the most important subject of Bellocq's photographs of New Orleans prostitutes, is located on a performative grid long before she poses for a photograph. As the object of a gaze that strips away the pretense of passing and circumscribes her within the space of racial and gendered *other*, Ophelia remembers the effort to acquire literacy as a vehicle of self-betterment rather than self-concealment.

As we move to "Vignette," we find Ophelia posing for Bellocq, an image of both exoticism and refinement. What drives the poem, however, is Trethewey's intimation that theirs is a collaborative relationship, not an exploitative one. This is not to suggest that they function on the same social plane, but rather to highlight Trethewey's technique of using the conceit of photographic composition as a way to turn the process inward. Which is to say that the photograph, posed outside a brothel with the aim of producing an image worthy of a gilded frame, is a prison whose destructiveness issues, not from its power to confine, but rather because it allows egress. Ophelia steps out of the fiction of the photograph back into the world of prostitution, where she is sexual commodity.

Thus, in looking at the poem "Bellocq's Ophelia" we see the juxtaposition of the painting representing Ophelia's death and Bellocq's photographs of her in life. The model, whose job is to approximate the moment of Ophelia's demise, is posed in a bathtub, "for hours, shivering / catching cold," the look on her face one of invitation and acquiescence. In a particularly deft act of conceptual overlay, Trethewey merges the two "Ophelias" and suggests that it does not matter which is real, ultimately, what is most important is a recognition of the symbolic economy at work here. For though the poem's speaker can hold both in her mind, the knowledge that the model stepped out of the bathtub and back into her life leads to the conclusion that the act of pulling "all movement from her slender limbs" into "her heavy-lidded eyes" is indicative of a female gaze, where the performative is likewise a blockage (note her lips are "poised to open, to speak," as if to suggest that the price of being visual subject is the forfeiture of speech). One can *appear ready* to speak, but the photographic image (as opposed to the cinematic image about to emerge at the time the poems are set) cannot breach the boundary between the visual and the aural.

What I have identified in each of the poems I have selected is an impulse on the part of the respective poets to enter the archives and use its contents as sources of creativity. Though any comparisons of the present moment in African American poetry and the Black Arts Movement are bound to be reductive, what I wish to point out is the manner in which we see a movement away from topicality as a determinant of poetic subject matter. This is not to say that African American poetry has relinquished its concerns about racial injustice or the contingent nature of life in America, but it is meant to suggest a continuity with, as opposed to a break from, the previous moment. For, in turning to the archives, African American poetry has taken up the clarion call issued in the 60s to reclaim the past. However, they have begun to repair the rent fabric of the past, not by restoring its facticity, which would mean that all poets would have to hew to the party line about a particular event, but rather by restoring the spirit of play within the context of history. Hence, two poets can write poems that partake of the same archival sources and produce — through semantics rather than aesthetics — radically different poems. Poets can, in turning to the archived image, do a great deal to interrogate the silences that inhere in cultural practices. Surely, this is a reason to rejoice, for if we have reached a point where the audience for poetry (however small) is secure in the notion of what Arnold Krupat calls "American Histories," then this anthology, with its diversity of voices and aesthetic realms, is a watershed in both name and deed.

WORKS CITED

Anderson, Benedict. *Imagined Communities*. London: Verso, 1983, rpt. 1991.

Brown, Michael. "History and History's Problem." *Social Text*. No. 16. Winter, 1986-87. 136-61.

DuPlessis, Rachel Blau. "Darken Your Speech: Racialized Cultural Work of Modernist Poets." *Reading Race in American Poetry*. Aldon Lynn Nielsen, ed. Urbana, IL: University of Illinois Press, 2000. 43-84.

Friedman, Susan Stanford. *Mappings: Feminism and the Cultural Geographies of Encounter*. Princeton, NJ: Princeton University Press, 1998.

Guillory, John. *Cultural Capital: The Problem of Literary Canon Formation*. Chicago: University of Chicago Press, 1993.

Hernadi, Paul. "Clio's Cousins: Historiography, Translation, Fiction and Criticism." *New Literary History*. Vol. 7, no. 2. Winter, 1976. 247-57.

Krupat, Arnold. "America's Histories." *American Literary History*. Vol. 10, no. 1. Spring, 1998. 124-46.

Mason, Theodore O. "The African American Anthology: Mapping the Territory, Taking the National Census, Building the Musuem." *American Literary History*. Vol. 10, no. 1. 185-98.

McFeely, William S. *Frederick Douglass.* New York: Touchstone Books, 1991.

Merelman, Richard. *Representing Black Culture: Racial Conflicts and Cultural Politics in the United States.* New York: Routledge, 1995.

Naylor, Paul. *Poetic Investigations: Singing the Holes in History.* Evanston, IL: Northwestern University Press, 1999.

Octalog (multiple authors). "The Politics of Historiography." *Rhetoric Review.* Vol. 7, no. 1. Autumn. 1988. 5-49.

Octalog II. "The Politics of Historiography." *Rhetoric Review.* Vol. 16, no. 1. Autumn. 1997. 22-44.

Smith, David. "The Black Arts Movement and Its Critics." *American Literary History.* Vol. 3, no. 1. Spring 1991. 93-110.

Trouillot, Michel-Rolph. *Silencing the Past: Power and the Production of History.* Boston: Beacon Press, 1995.

Kathy Lou Schultz

SMALL PRESS, BIG WOR(L)DS: AFRICAN AMERICAN POETRY FROM PUBLISHER TO ARCHIVE

In an interview first published in *The Washington Post* in 1973 in which he was asked about black vernacular traditions, Ralph Ellison quipped: "I'm sure that the Afro has killed off more folklore than anything else, because guys don't have to go to the barbershop or stay there long enough for the lying to start" (West, 39). With this statement, Ellison marks the dynamic, living nature of folkloric practices rooted in African American vernacular. Black folklore is not a subject to be dusted off by well-meaning scholars; rather, vernacular practices continue to form and reform contemporary black culture. In 21st century America, Ellison's proverbial barbershop remains central in many communities, where patrons often seek not only a shape-up but also an interactive linguistic event. Young boys listen and observe for years before being allowed to participate in "grown folks' talk" and so a ritual of growing into black manhood is sustained. In lamenting the passage of dialect from African American poetry early in the 20th century, Henry Louis Gates, Jr. writes: "Because dialect was an independent form it could carry independent meaning — a distinctively black meaning." Surely the barbershop remains in some neighborhoods as an independent locale for the production of "distinctively black meaning" (183). This meaning takes the form of both physical and linguistic signs. Young men with elaborate plats or Afros are signifying as loudly through hairstyles as through what is called dialect. For the literary critic wary of essentializing blackness, awareness of such sites of independent black meaning unto themselves (as well as in their relation to dominant white culture) remains important.

Keeping in mind interventions concerning the constructions of race,[1] I want to draw attention to the work of contemporary African American poets whose poetics are attuned to both life and language,

[1] Paul Gilroy in *The Black Atlantic* cautions against the danger of "leaving racial essentialism behind by viewing 'race' itself as a social and cultural construction." This tendency, Gilroy warns, "has been insufficiently alive to the lingering power of specifically racialised forms of power and subordination" (32).

without seeing language as merely transparent, as I explore contemporary reading and publishing practices. These poets, who are part of a continuing lineage of African American modernism, such as Nathaniel Mackey, Harryette Mullen, Erica Hunt, C. S. Giscombe, and Will Alexander, are followed by a younger generation including Renee Gladman and giovanni singleton. These poets understand what has come to be called the materiality of language, while placing that material within specifically African American contexts. In attempting to define those contexts, however, critics can court a world of trouble. Critics such as Paul Gilroy may be wary of the possibility that liberal definitions of race become so broad that race itself can seem to mean both everything and nothing. If race is only a signifier on the page, racialized forms of power and subordination may seem belittled, ignored. However, when poets and critics attempt to define blackness too narrowly, or see blackness as an unchanging, essentialist identity, large groups of poets are pushed off the map (or page, or anthology).

As Gates pointed out in an argument published more than twenty years ago, but still of critical importance, African Americanist criticism has suffered from a privileging of content over form, when "experience" is the critic's defining lens. Black texts, he writes:

> were generally analyzed almost exclusively in terms of their content, as if a literary form were a vacant enclosure that would be filled with this or that matter. This matter, moreover, was "the Black Experience," and an author tended to be judged on his or her fidelity to "the Black Experience." This, it seemed to me, was a dead end for black literary studies. (xxii)

These reading practices have caused important black writers such as Melvin Tolson to be ignored until very recently because Tolson's writing demonstrates his commitment to a modernist poetic tradition, one which in Tolson's hands continually investigates and complicates readings of black identity.

Indeed, we have only begun to recognize the continuation of African

American modernism that leads to today's innovative poetic practices. As Nathaniel Mackey pointed out at a conference on innovation and African American writing hosted by Small Press Traffic in San Francisco in 2000, "Racialized dichotomies between content and form, accessibility and difficulty, conventionality and innovation and so forth rest on a division of cultural labor black experimental writing has to contest and overcome" (8). Indeed, because of tendencies to read African American poetry "separately," Mackey had trouble finding a publisher for his book of criticism, *Discrepant Engagement*, which deals with experimental writing by African American, white American, and Caribbean authors. One university press informed him that "the book's problem is that it's not really one book but potentially three: a book on experimental writing, a book on African American writing, and a book on Caribbean writing" (8). Note that the publisher's supposedly neutral-sounding category "experimental writing" actually means "white experimental writing" because the writers in the study of other racial and national identities are pulled out into separate categories. This way of separating poets by racial identity also obscures the influence that writers have on one another across racial lines. Often this means that the influence that African Americans have on the American canon are elided. For example, Aldon Nielsen demonstrates the ways in which the poets of the Umbra group "can be seen as the unacknowledged forerunners to the L=A=N=G=U=A=G=E poets" (113).

There do remain compelling reasons, however, to consider African American literature as a category as well. Some students may not be aware that programs such as Africana Studies or Women's Studies were not granted benevolently; rather activists demanded that such perspectives be taught, and many of the conditions necessitating those fights remain. Without an awareness of African American history, it is impossible to appreciate works such as Anthony Walton's "McDonald's, Scottsboro, April ,1997" in which the "pink / and silver-ringed fingers" of "the white girl" who appears in the first line of the poem call to mind the danger that racist/sexist constructions of white female sexuality (as pure) and black male sexuality (as predatorial) pose to black men.

When the so-called Scottsboro Boys were dragged off a freight train near Scottsboro, Alabama and into history in 1931, a touchstone of American history became brutally clear: it takes the word of only one white woman (the other later recanted) to condemn nine black men. Walton writes that her "fingers touch mine — / so benign, as if time / and the town were / as innocent as she."

In addition, African Americans have a unique historical relationship to writing and literacy because of the conditions enforced in slavery, including the fact that it was illegal for a slave to learn to read and write. In a continuing engagement with this history, both Evie Shockley and Timothy Seibles imagine letters written by Frederick Douglass, author of one of the most famous "literacy as freedom" texts. (Notably, both poems investigate Douglass's relationship with Ottilie Assing, a German Jewish woman with whom Douglass had an affair.) As Gates documents, African American writers including Douglass faced the burden of proving reason, indeed their very humanity, through literacy.

In attempts to first locate (uncover, recover) and then to define an African American literary tradition, contemporary critics often turn to the vernacular roots of black culture. This is a prospect marked with a great deal of complexity and contradiction, but work in this area has helped to demonstrate black contributions to the American literary canon. Again it is important here not to label black culture as singularly oral in nature (many other cultures have strong oral traditions and African peoples have historically possessed writing systems) or to define black vernacularity too rigidly. Perhaps demonstrating the problem of defining blackness in such a way as to seem to contain both everything and nothing, Fahamisha Patricia Brown in *Performing the Word: African American Poetry as Vernacular Culture* states: "I use the term *African American vernacular culture* to refer to those customs and mores that appear to be most specifically manifested by persons in the United States who trace their ancestry to Africans enslaved there" (28). Almost anything could fit into this category. Brown goes on to focus on specific vernacular practices such as the boast, "rappin'" and the sermon, but her history of African American poetry does not include any of the poets in the black modernist lineage that I have begun to sketch out above, though these writers certainly engage black vernacular on a number of levels.

This is a continuing problem of omission in scholarly narratives of African American poetry and other poetic traditions associated with identity. African American poets who engage in what is called experimental or innovative writing practices following from a modernist tradition may be doubly marginalized by race and aesthetics. Innovative African American women poets face additional challenges due to gender.

> [W]omen's contributions to experimental poetry publication today are not well recognized in current scholarly narratives. Because American academic feminism has generally allied itself with an identity politics focus, and because the greatest impetus for reading, teaching, and publishing works by women has come from feminist scholars, the view from academe tends to obscure women's publishing that does not fit this mold. (Keller and Miller)

The division between African American poetry described as innovative and other African American poetry thought to be more conventional continues to affect reading and publishing practices. In some respects, the state of publishing in African American poetry reflects the situation of American poetry in general, including the vital role that small presses headed by poet/publishers play, while in other respects we must consider the historical conditions that affect African American poetry in particular.

For example, without the editorial work of African American writers such as Langston Hughes and Arna Bontemps, Stephen Henderson, or LeRoi Jones/Amiri Baraka and Larry Neal who worked as anthologists, our access to the rich and varied history of African American writing would be sorely limited. Given the history in the U.S. of white anthology editors who employed the "one at a time" method in which one African American poet was utilized as representative, black writers have also necessarily acted as editors and publishers of African

American writing. Some of the publishing projects that grew out of the energy and commitments of the Black Arts Movement that spawned so many anthologies continue today. For example, Third World Press, founded by Haki R. Madhubuti (Don L. Lee) in 1967 with the help of Johari Amini (Jewel C. Latimore) and Carolyn Rodgers, continues to publish about a dozen books by black writers per year. Younger African American writers such as giovanni singleton have also launched publications. singleton edits and publishes her own journal called *Nocturnes*, the first issue of which appeared in 2001, which contains a substantial amount of work by African American writers.

Today, much of the most dynamic contemporary African American poetry is published by such small presses as these, as well as others run by non-black editors. Small press publishers with a specific commitment to socially marginalized women writers have published many African American women early in their careers. Some of these presses sprang from the feminist publishing movement in the 1970s. Kelsey St. Press, for instance, founded by poet/editors Patricia Dienstfrey and Rena Rosenwasser, who continue to direct the press, has been in existence since 1974 and its current commitments to "experimental work by emerging writers, women of color, and lesbians" suggest its origins in the feminist movement. With a focus on "innovative writing by women" Kelsey St. describes its origins as follows: "Our genesis was a group of writers who felt compelled to address the historical marginalization of women writers by mainstream publishers" (Press History). Young African American poet and experimental prose writer Renee Gladman has thus far published all of her books and chapbooks with small presses in the San Francisco Bay Area, including Kelsey St. which published *Juice* in 2000. In addition to her writing, Renee Gladman also conducts her own publishing projects. She is the former editor of *Clamour*, a journal dedicated to experimental writing by women of color, and from 1999 to 2004, she was editor and publisher of a chapbook imprint, *LEROY*, which she founded to publish emerging and geographically obscured writers. She is currently publishing *Leona*, a pamphlet series of experimental prose and poetry, and *Leon Works*, a perfect-bound series for full-length prose works. These small presses are uniquely positioned to represent local aesthetic communities, as well as to publish younger writers before other presses are aware of their work.

Other small presses that have published important works of African American poetry are run by multi-racial editorial teams of poet/editors under 40. Indeed, many young poets work in editorial teams comprised of members who represent different racial, gender, and sexual identities. In addition to her Kelsey St. book, Gladman has published collections with Idiom and Krupskaya, two such presses. Begun in Berkeley, California around 1994, the principal members of Idiom's "ever influx collective" included Pamela Lu, Adam DeGraff, and Alex Corey (Lu, RE: Idiom Press). In a talk given at the Page Mother's conference at the University of California, San Diego, Lu describes the "half a dozen or so editors": "Many of us had met as students at Berkeley where we had been influenced by developments inspired by Language Poetry and the New York School, as well as revisions of canonical authorship, criticism, and art." Krupskaya Press was founded and financed by Jocelyn Saidenberg in 1998; the first editorial collective members were Saidenberg, Rodrigo Toscano, and Hung Q. Tu. Though Krupskaya has no stated ideology concerning the gender or race of the poets it publishes, innovative writers of color, including young African American poets, are routinely part of their list. Krupskaya also published Tyrone Williams's first book-length collection, *c.c.*.

Mary Burger's Second Story Press, which also issued a chapbook by Renee Gladman, is described variously as focusing on "cross-genre narrative/lyrical works,"[2] and "short works of experimental narrative"[3] indicating younger writers' continuing interest in works that cross traditional genre boundaries. Her interest in formally experimental work mirrors that of Singing Horse Press, the influential small press run by Gil Ott from Philadelphia for more than 20 years until his untimely death in 2004. Singing Horse published *Muse & Drudge* (1995) and *S*PeRM**K*T* (1992), two collections by Harryette Mullen that continue to be extremely popular. All of Mullen's early books, including the groundbreaking prose poem set *Trimmings* (Tender

[2] http://www.sfsu.edu/~poetry/narrativity/about_editors.html
[3] http://www.frenchcx.com/english/MARYBURGER.htm

Buttons 1991; out of print), were published by small presses. Black writers, like many American poets, often follow a trajectory from small press to university press in their publishing careers. Mullen has two in-print poetry collections from university presses: *Sleeping With the Dictionary* (2002) is part of the New California Poetry Series published by the University of California Press, and *Blues Baby: Early Poems* (2002) is one of the Bucknell Series in Contemporary Poetry.[4] Some readers incorrectly interpret university press publication as a sort of arrival or legitimation, but Mullen's earlier small press works *Muse & Drudge* and *Trimmings* were not simply preparation for later university press publications. On the contrary, *Muse & Drudge* and *Trimmings* are essential Afro-Modernist innovations sharing a lineage as much with Sterling Brown as with Gertrude Stein.

While small press publishing indicates the vast amount of cultural work being performed by contemporary poets, problems remain in preserving this work for history. Vast numbers of texts pass hand to hand throughout writing communities that, though widely read, do not have ISBN or ISSN numbers, or do not end up in research libraries. Here the difference between independent press and university press publications shows itself: university press publications are more likely to end up on library shelves. Libraries may place standing orders for university press poetry series, while other series simply may not be on the radar. When a book goes out of print or is no longer available through a distributor such as Small Press Distribution in Berkeley, California, future readers may never come across it. Even well-intentioned researchers may never come in contact with some important works unless they have access to those particular writing communities. After publishing an essay on African American poet Erica Hunt in the web journal *HOW2*, I was contacted by other researchers wishing to know more about Hunt's work, but unable to get their hands on certain texts. As of September 2004, two of Hunt's works are available for sale

---

[4] For a different trajectory, consider Nathaniel Mackey's career: though Mackey's *Eroding Witness*, a National Poetry Series selection in 1984, published by the University of Illinois Press, is considered his first book, he published two small press book before it (*Four for Trane*, Golemics, 1978; and *Septet for the End of Time*, Boneset/Hambone, 1983). After being selected for the National Poetry Series, his subsequent books of poetry and experimental fiction have appeared in a variety of small press formats, from a limited edition, saddle-stitched chapbook from Chax Press (*Four for Glenn*, 2002) to inclusion in the Sun & Moon Classics series (*Bedouin Hornbook*, 1997).

through Small Press Distribution: *Arcade* (Kelsey St., 1996) and *Piece Logic* (Carolina Wren Press, 2002). *Local History*, published by Roof Books of the Segue Foundation in New York City in 1993, is out of print, but is available as an e-book downloadable from the publisher's website. However, a visit to my home research library at the University of Pennsylvania reveals to my disappointment that they currently own none of Hunt's books.[5]

Small presses themselves have recognized the importance of maintaining archives, as Roof Books notes on its website detailing the activities of the Segue Foundation: "The Segue Distribution Archive is a special collection of several thousand rare and hard-to-find small press books and journals based on the Foundation's 13 year tenure (1980–1993) as a major non-profit literary distributor." The Archive is housed in the foundation's office in New York City and is open to the public for viewing by appointment. Black Sparrow, publisher of several works by Wanda Coleman including *Bathwater Win*e, winner of the 1999 Lenore Marshall Prize in Poetry from the Academy of American Poets, has portions of its archive housed in several university libraries. All of the documentation related to the storied Southern California press's first 94 collections, from "the first publication of [Charles] Bukowski's broadside *True Story* in April, 1966 to those related to Gerard Malanga's volume *Ten Poems for Ten Poets,* published in November, 1970" are housed at the University of Alberta (O'Driscoll, "Contents"). "Further Black Sparrow Press materials are held at the Special Collections Department of Pennsylvania State University (1967-1974); the Center for Southwest Research at the University of New Mexico (1967-1975); Special Collections at the University of Arizona (1973-1993), and the University of California at Berkeley (1993-present)" (O'Driscoll, "Provenance").

In areas of African American cultural production other than poetry, such as music, those works labeled variously as underground, alternative, or independent are not only on the radar of readers, listeners, and critics, but such works are often prized. These manifestations of the local, similar to folkloric practices handed down at the neighborhood

---

[5] SUNY Buffalo owns *Local History, Arcade*, and *Piece Logic*. They are all housed in Poetry/Rare Books, a non-circulating collection. University of California–San Diego also has these books in its Archive for New Poetry, another "library use only" archive.

barbershop, have in the academy come under the purview of cultural studies as well as other disciplines. When reading poetry we must learn to recognize the importance of the local as well, and that cultural work is being published by small presses. As we investigate contemporary poetry, we must understand that simply looking for a university press imprint is not easy shorthand for locating importance or quality. (Important works emerge from a variety of presses including those that are independent and those affiliated with universities.) However, we must not be deceived into thinking that there are two easily discernible aesthetics divided into small press and university press categories.[6] In fact, one would be hard-pressed to define an aesthetic under a label such as "academic poetry." As Lorenzo Thomas stated in the Diversity in African American Poetry Conference's keynote, "there is no longer a category of 'academic poetry' in American letters" (200). Indeed if we were to assemble a group of poets who attended the conference who might be called academic poets by virtue of being full-time members of the professoriate or publishing with university presses, there is no way to sensibly generalize their work. For example, Honorée Fanonne Jeffers does not write like Nathaniel Mackey who does not write like Anthony Walton who does not write like C. S. Giscombe and so on.

But if there is not such a division between the writers, there may be between readers. I would go so far as to conjecture that the majority of readers who support contemporary poetry through such activities as attending readings, or purchasing magazines or chapbooks, are not academics. The active poet/critic is a notable exception, but while it is not easy to get a PhD English, it is easy to get one without knowing a thing about 20th century American poetry. Criticism, too, lags behind poetic practice. This concerns me because, as a poet, I know that the making of literary history is a lot messier than literary criticism leads one to believe. As a critic, I am beguiled when I read a great theory, a newly invented chronology, but I worry: is that the way it really was? The formation of literary history is often an outgrowth of social relationships, marriages and divorces, political alliances and enemies,

---

[6] I have not even begun to address the politics of commercial publishing, which is outside the scope of this essay, though commercial presses certainly share an aesthetic preference for works perceived as marketable and therefore profitable.

chance friendships and chosen allegiances, manifestations of the local that belie the critic's categories and construction of linear narratives. Through meticulous use of poets' personal papers, some critics are able to reconstruct past networks that form the basis of key moments in literary history. For example, Aldon Nielsen's research into Amiri Baraka's papers allowed him to trace literary networks formed through Baraka by important (yet mostly neglected) post-WWII African American poets such as Ray Bremser and Harold Carrington (84-96). Yet when archivists in the future ask for a poet's papers, what will be in the box? Will all the emails have been deleted? So look now, look hard. Such awareness of local cultural production could lead you to a fantastic poetry reading or a really great haircut. You just have to read the signs.[7]

WORKS CITED

"About Us." *Roof Books*. 2004. The Segue Foundation. 13 Sept. 2004. <http://www.roofbooks.com/Segue/>.

Brown, Fahamisha Patricia. *Performing the Word: African American Poetry as Vernacular Culture.* New Brunswick: Rutgers UP, 1999.

Gates, Henry Louis, Jr. *Figures in Black: Words, Signs, and the Racial Self.* New York: Oxford UP, 1987.

Gilroy, Paul. *The Black Atlantic: Modernity and Double Consciousness.* Cambridge: Harvard UP, 1993.

Keller, Lynn and Cristanne Miller. "Gender and Avant-Garde Editing: Comparing the 1920s with the 1990s." *HOW2 — Contemporary Innovative Writing by Women* Vol. 1, No. 2, September 1999. 13 Sept. 2004 <http://www.scc.rutgers.edu/however/v1_2_1999/current/readings/keller-miller.html>.

[7] I would like to thank: Keith Tuma and Herman Beavers for inviting me to write this essay; Bob Perelman, Jessica Lowenthal, and Robin Tremblay-McGaw for reading drafts; and Brian Slaughter for sharing his barbershop anecdotes as well as daily support.

Lu, Pamela. "Re: Idiom Press." E-mail to the author. 8 Sept. 2004.

---. "*Idiom*: A Story of Anti-Production, or The Triumph of Sloth." *HOW2 — Contemporary Innovative Writing by Women* Vol. 1, No. 2, September 1999. <http://www.scc.rutgers.edu/however/v1_2_1999/current/readings/lu.html>.

Mackey, Nathaniel. "Expanding the Repertoire." *Tripwire: A Journal of Poetics* 5 (2001): 7-10.

Nielsen, Aldon. *Black Chant: Languages of African American Postmodernism.* New York: Cambridge UP, 1997.

O'Driscoll, Michael and Jason Dewinetz. "Contents of the Archive." *Black Sparrow Press Archive.* May 2002. University of Alberta. 13 Sept, 2004 <http://www.uofaweb.ualberta.ca/bsp/nav01.cfm?nav01=15375>.

---. "Provenance of the Archive." *Black Sparrow Press Archive.* May 2002. University of Alberta. 13 Sept. 2004 <http://www.uofaweb.ualberta.ca/bsp/nav01.cfm?nav01=15374>.

"Press History." *Kelsey St. Press — Poetry by Women.* 13 Sept. 2004 <http://www.kelseyst.com/history.htm>.

"Third World Press History." *Third World Press.* 1 September 2004. <http://www.thirdworldpressinc.com/history.htm>.

West, Hollie. "Travels with Ralph Ellison Through Time and Thought." *Speaking for You: The Vision of Ralph Ellison.* Kimberly W. Benston, Ed. Washington, D.C.: Howard UP, 1990. 37-44.

Lorenzo Thomas

OUR HERITAGE OF MANY VOICES: DIVERSITY IN AFRICAN AMERICAN POETRY

Plenary Address

This is a conference on poetry; so let me begin with a poem. This is called "Slim Greer" by the great folklorist, literary critic, teacher, and — he would say — liar, Sterling A. Brown. "Slim Greer" is about a fellow who is a waiter by occupation and — like Sterling Brown — a conversationalist by profession.

Listen to the tale
Of Ole Slim Greer,
Waitines' devil
Waitin' here

Talkinges' guy
An' biggest liar
With always a new lie
On the fire.

Tells a tale
Of Arkansaw
That keeps the kitchen
In a roar;

Tells in a long-drawled
Careless tone,
As solemn as a Baptist
Parson's moan.

How he in Arkansaw
Passed for white,
An' he no lighter
Than a dark midnight.

Found a nice white woman
At a dance,
Thought he was from Spain
Or else from France;

Nobody suspicioned
Ole Slim Greer's race
But a Hill Billy always
Roun' the place,

Who called one day
On the trustful dame
An' found Slim comfy
When he came.

The whites lef' the parlor
All to Slim
Which didn't cut
No ice with him,

An' he started a-tinklin'
Some mo'nful blues,
An' a-pattin' the time
With No. Fourteen shoes.

The cracker listened
An' then he spat
An' said, "No white man
Could play like that..."

The point of the poem, of course, is that we live in a society where — until quite recently — unless it was otherwise stipulated, everyone was assumed to be white. In fact, before 1960, big city newspapers in the South never printed any items about black people unless they were involved in crimes (which would include, of course, all of those ministers and school children who packed Southern jails in the 1950s).

Clearly, this assumption of whiteness has been reflected in our literature and other cultural expressions as well. If you think that "Slim Greer" is actually about music, then it might occur to you that Brown is somehow celebrating what W. E. B. Du Bois called the African's gift of song to American culture; that the poem indeed turns on the unique qualities of African American folk music — and the sophisticated forms derived from it — that we celebrate as authentic expressions of blackness.

And, yes, you would be right. But in the American historical context, the other face of *authenticity* is *exclusion*.

As far as poetry is concerned, we can see that, beginning in 1900, many anthologies of American poetry included only one or two poets who happened to be African American, regardless of what style of poetry they produced. And, in 1950, F. O. Mattheissen's influential *Oxford Book of American Poetry* admitted no black American writer at all (Golding 27).

For those who could look past the assumption of whiteness, who did manage to see that black poets did, in fact, exist — there was still a problem. As Alan Golding has suggested, "opposing definitions of 'black poetry' were in place by 1849" with one definition simply marking any poetry written by African American writers as black poetry, and the other definition focused on poetry offering "racial themes" (27).

The vexing situation with African American poetry is that on one hand, because of its connection to a unique oral tradition, it has been a locus of stylistic and formal innovation. On the other hand, critics have persisted in characterizing black poets who choose to work in traditional or current poetic styles as derivative, imitative, or — if they do it very well — "uppity."

Hidden in Plain View

The perception that the African American poet who simply works in the prevailing poetic idiom of her time is somehow out of place is, of course, a corollary of that "assumption of whiteness" mentioned earlier. It has certainly been reflected in criticism of African American poetry since the beginning of the 20th century.

In some ways, the way that we have theorized this dichotomy mirrors the distinction that Robert Lowell made in 1960 describing the prevailing approaches to American poetry as "the cooked and the raw." Commenting on the turf war of that era between the Beats and the academic poets, Lowell noted, "There is a poetry that can only be studied, and a poetry that can only be declaimed, a poetry of pedantry and a poetry of scandal" (quoted in Golding 28).

Lowell exaggerated for effect, of course. But, even though there is no longer a category of "academic poetry" in American letters, we have witnessed a similar dichotomy in discussions of black poetry in recent years. It has been assumed that there is an authentic black poetry — though it has proved difficult to define its properties. Yet we have also continued to suffer from invisibility.

In 1925, reviewing early anthologies of African American poets edited by Robert T. Kerlin and by Newman Ivy White, Guy B. Johnson recalled a strange incident:

> A few months ago I was discussing books of poetry with a professor of English in one of the largest colleges in the Southwest. He happened to say that he was using one of William Stanley Braithwaite's anthologies in his course on modern poetry. I remarked that I considered it a sign of progress that Southern white teachers were using books compiled by leading Negro poets. He was indignant: Braithwaite could not possibly be a Negro, and that was final. (315)

He adds:

> I did not press my point, knowing that it might have led to a complete revolution in his course on modern poetry, so he probably believes still that Braithwaite is a hundred percent white, Anglo-Saxon, Protestant, native-born American. (315)

Braithwaite, of course, was African American. Best known as the editor of the annual *Anthology of Magazine Verse* beginning in 1913, Braithwaite was an important critic in the 1920s. Hailed by J. Max Barber's *Voice of the Negro* in 1908 as Dunbar's successor — not because of his subject matter, but because of his poetic skill — Braithwaite did not include "racial themes" in his own poetry. Braithwaite's "universality" apparently sold a few books to those who assumed he was white, but it also brought him a critical drubbing from J. Saunders Redding. In his groundbreaking volume *To Make a Poet Black* (1939), Redding dismissed Braithwaite's efforts as "the most outstanding example of perverted energy that the period from 1903 to 1917 produced" (Thomas 70).

This afternoon I'd like to talk a little about another poet who could not pass for white; a poet who was the first major star of the Harlem Renaissance. Quiet as it's kept, this is his centennial year.

I'm talking about Countee Cullen (1903-1946).

It is a terrible thing to be present and "unseen;" but what our literature tells us about how we *were* seen can be just as troubling.

We know that the Harlem Renaissance of the 1920s was a tremendous outpouring of black creativity; often celebrating the kind of racial authenticity that Sterling Brown teases us about in "Slim Greer." But it might be useful to consider what — besides Jim Crow laws — the New Negro was up against.

In *The Souls of Black Folk* (1903), W. E. B. Du Bois pointed out how awful it was to be seen not in human terms but as a political or sociological issue; how demeaning it was to be asked, almost daily, "How does it feel to be a problem?"

Two decades later things had not improved very much — even among the intellectuals who read Du Bois's books. How black Americans were perceived as profoundly unalterably Other is revealed in *Poetry* magazine's January 1926 review of folklorist Dorothy Scarborough's *On the Trail of Negro Folk-Songs.*

"Long before finishing Miss Scarborough's book," writes Eda Lou Walton,

> one becomes convinced that the Negro is America's best ballad-singer, that his emotional heritage has made him the most *natural* of poets. Although the author has chosen her title to suggest her method; to me it has a deeper significance. It reminds me of the Navajo cry for opening the medicine ceremonies: "On the trail of the Singer of Songs, come!" a command to the gods to come down to a suffering people. I believe that the Negro too may have the feeling that his song bridges the gap between the supernatural and natural worlds. (Walton 223; emphasis added)

Noting the similarity to Native American religious chants would also remind some readers that — in American literature beginning with Washington Irving in the 1820s, reinforced by federal government policies beginning in the 1830s — the Indians belonged to a vanishing species. So, too — at least according to Prudential Insurance Company actuary Frederick J. Hoffman in the 1890s — did black Americans.

Still, perceptive listeners might find Miss Walton's analogy a bit off-key. Those black folk were singing about Jesus, weren't they?

Well, that won't get you out of the box either, Mr. Osiris. "The Spirituals," Miss Walton declares, "express the Negro's pitiful adoption of Christianity as a suitable religion for sufferers" (224).

If you understand that, then perhaps you will also understand why the officials at Bob Jones University, until quite recently forbade their white Christian students to date black Christian students.

When Miss Walton nevertheless concludes that the spirituals might be the world's most beautiful music (226), this echo of statements made much earlier by W. E. B. Du Bois and James Weldon Johnson sounds hollow indeed.

Miss Walton's image of the African American as Other is precisely what Alain Locke's 1925 anthology *The New Negro* was intended to correct. But the pervasiveness of the image is remarkable.

Writing in *Phylon*, Robert A. Smith informs us that, in 1928, *Poet Lore* editor Gertrude Thornhill,

> considering [Countee] Cullen's work, wrote that the Negro, because of his "sorrow and suffering," because he is "humble," may soon make a great contribution to American literature. (216)

We might notice that Thornhill did not actually mean that Cullen might make a great contribution. She was speaking of the generic Negro.

"The fallacy in her statement," Smith comments somewhat peevishly, "lies in the fact that all of the Negroes and Negro poets do not fit this description. Countee Cullen did not typify the 'humble,' singing Negro. His training, scholarship, and Phi Beta Kappa key would hardly leave him with any such complex."

Indeed, Smith points out, Cullen "enjoyed being the most highly educated and most distinguished of his contemporary Negro poets" (216).

Cullen was fabulously successful at the beginning of his career — but he died much too early and has not received as much critical attention as he deserves.

As the poems collected in his first volume, *Color* (1925), testify, Cullen did have a problem directly related to race. "Cullen was keenly aware of, and sensitive to, the problem of discrimination," writes Smith, "although the arts are sometimes free of it. As he stated, there was forever the problem of being made black and bidden to sing. He found this an insurmountable obstacle; it was difficult for him to fight successfully with his pen" (221).

Again, J. Saunders Redding in *To Make a Poet Black* — his 1939 historical survey of African American poetry, its title taken from Cullen's sonnet "Yet Do I Marvel" — saw the same problem but analyzed it differently. Redding argues that

> undoubtedly the biggest, single unalterable circumstance in the life of Mr. Cullen is his color. Most of the life he has lived has been influenced by it. And when he writes by it, he *writes*; but when this does not guide him, his pen trails faded ink across his pages. (109)

And it is true that when Cullen writes about the effects of racial discrimination he produces passionate, astonishing poems. It is also true that he expended a great deal of effort attempting to restrain this passion — just as described in his poem "Heritage."

Redding points out that Cullen's *Caroling Dusk* (1927), "his anthology of 'verse by Negro poets,' represents a careful culling of the less distinctive, that is to say, the less Negroid poetry of his most defiantly Negro contemporaries" (108).

Redding also hints that the traditional English-language stanza forms favored by Cullen and other Harlem Renaissance poets were chosen for a similar motive. In *To Make a Poet Black*, Redding notes that Jean Toomer's *Cane* (1923) was an avant-garde experiment that did not set an attractive *formal* precedent. Instead, Redding claims, *Cane*

> established the precedent of self-revelation that has characterized the writings of Negroes on all levels ever since. At first completely absorbed in fulfilling his opportunity for [emotional] release, the New Negro had no time for new forms. In his anxiety and relief he did not reflect that he was pouring new wine into old bottles. In truth, he was somewhat distrustful of his new place in the sun. He was afraid of being a fad, the momentary focus of the curiosity of dilettantes, charlatans, and student sociologists. (105-106)

But with Countee Cullen, it is obvious that the choice of poetic form is a crucial matter.

In 1925, Harlem was "in vogue" but African American leaders

were not entirely happy about it. Consuela Francis writes

> Something had gone grievously wrong with the master plan — instead of revealing something of African American experience that might lead to an objective understanding of black difference, African Americans were becoming an exotic curiosity. (52)

In other words, what Redding said they'd most feared had come true. She adds that the *Crisis* magazine symposium "The Negro in Art" (1926), and essays by Langston Hughes and George Schuyler in *The Nation*, reflect "the effort to figure where things went wrong" (Francis 52).

The *Crisis* symposium was convened to address a serious problem of representation. The editors wrote that "while the individual portrait may be true and artistic, the net result in American literature to date is to picture twelve million Americans as prostitutes, thieves, and fools" (quoted in Francis 52).

In a society where the most familiar depictions of black folk would have been *Birth of a Nation* at one extreme and the novel that gave us *Porgy and Bess* at the sympathetic end, the most fascinating of the symposium's seven questions is probably still relevant today:

> Can publishers be criticized for refusing to handle novels that portray Negroes of education and accomplishment, on the ground that these characters are no different from white folk and therefore not interesting?

Yep, there's that issue of *authenticity* again.

Countee Cullen, of course, broadcast his own image of education and accomplishment and enjoyed being a poet whose public recognition rivaled Edna St. Vincent Millay's. As a poet he insisted that while his subject matter might focus on African American life, his poetry was nevertheless part of a long English-language literary tradition. He argued that the African American writer had more to gain from study of that literature than from "any nebulous atavistic yearnings toward an African influence." Though his own poem "Heritage" (1925) includes a bit of it, Cullen definitely opposed the popular tendency among many poets at the time to indulge in sensationalized "primitive" imagery.

As editor of the anthology *Caroling Dusk,* Cullen intended to "represent" in the proper manner while attempting to demonstrate what he saw as diversity. He praised Anne Spencer's "cool precision," delighted in Lewis Alexander's experiments with haiku, and admired McKay's rebelliousness even though he feared it sometimes "clouds his lyricism." Above all, though, Cullen desired to "maintain the higher traditions of English verse."

Cullen, of course, was aware of the ambivalence of his own position. In his magnificent poem "Heritage" identifying himself as "one three centuries removed," Cullen wonders "what is Africa to me?" Self-doubt, social ostracism because of race, and skepticism about religious faith become powerfully conflicting forces. As with Du Bois's famous formulation of "double consciousness" in *The Souls of Black Folk*, Cullen shows how the discrepancy between Americans' democratic rhetoric and the realities of race threaten to mentally unhinge black citizens.

In "Pagan Prayer" (1925), Cullen frames the situation in a manner that, unlike the self-absorbed "Heritage," directly challenges American society:

> Our Father, God, our Brother, Christ —
> So are we taught to pray;
> Their kinship seems a little thing
> Who sorrow all the day.
>
> Our Father, God; our Brother, Christ,
> Or are we bastard kin,
> That to our plaints your ears are closed,
> Your doors barred from within?
>
> (Cullen 91)

And this is a challenge that would echo a half-century later in the poems of the Black Arts Movement.

Because the formalism of Cullen and Claude McKay was balanced by the vernacular innovation of Langston Hughes and Sterling Brown, the Harlem Renaissance did not, in fact, impose a stylistic or ideological uniformity upon poets. Some critics have argued, however, that the Black Arts Movement of the late 1960s and 1970s did.

Indeed, when it comes to the Black Arts Movement, there has been much less actual literary criticism than characterization. We constantly meet students who have been told that the Black Arts Movement was anti-Semitic, homophobic, and misogynistic. Despite the fact that two of the three best-selling poets of the era were women, these students have also been taught to believe that women were "silenced" by the Black Arts Movement.

If Redding was right to call the Renaissance an exercise in pouring new wine into old bottles, then the Black Arts Moment might be an instance of pouring old African American rhetorical practices into the new bottles of Projective verse prosody. As Regina Jennings has written, Black Arts Movement poets

> understood that if they were to redirect Black thinking, they would have to make Black people face personal, negative cultural assumptions. [Haki] Madhubiuti and the others sought through poetry to eradicate the idea of Black as evil in the collective Negro-becoming-Black consciousness. (109)

Those who chose to deliver such messages to the masses often ended up sounding just as preachy as the real preachers they distrusted and sometimes denounced.

In some ways, though, the Black Arts Movement was a spur toward a level of poetic diversity that had not previously been seen. That was partly because of its nationwide range and partly because of the issues of racial identity that it foregrounded. In her recently published work *The Feminist Avant-Garde in American Poetry* (2003), Elisabeth A. Frost usefully demonstrates that we must not look to simplistic dichotomies if we would fully grasp the importance of contemporary African American poetry. Sonia Sanchez, writes Frost,

> writes at the intersection of a number of competing identities: that of a black writer for whom feminist concerns were often suppressed in the interests of racial unity; that of an experimental writer whose early efforts were to score the space of the page as musical composition (and in this way exert the influence of the black vernacular and performance in a written medium); and that of an emerging black *feminist* writer who explored Black female subjectivity. (66)

In her discussion, Frost gives Sanchez the close and perceptive reading such multi-dimensionality both deserves and requires.

At *this* moment what can be said is that the diversity in stylistic approaches offered by African American poets provides a rich cornucopia for readers — from the plain spoken elegance of Lucille Clifton to the clever magic of Tyrone Williams's *c.c.* (2002), the intriguing play of persona and history in Kevin Young's *To Repel Ghosts* (2000) and *Jelly Roll* (2002), and the liberating linguistic innovations of Harryette Mullen's *Muse and Drudge* (1995) and *Sleeping with the Dictionary* (2002).

This is not to slight another half dozen poets whose *first* books are nothing less than astounding in quality and intelligence.

What we can say at this point is that African American poetry has continued to develop in two directions. There still remains a tension between the oral tradition — so highly valorized from Du Bois in the 1890s to the present day — and those who are interested in exploiting their inheritance of the English-language literary tradition.

We're talking about what comes with growing up in America. I think that I do agree with Countee Cullen: Keats and jazz and kung fu movies are as much a part of the heritage of African American poets as they are for Native American, Asian American, or Euro-American poets.

We can also see that what goes on between these two poles of the oral tradition and the literary tradition has become ever more interesting.

For example, what is today popularly termed "Spoken Word" can be seen as a very interesting development of Black Arts Movement poetic techniques.

If you pay close attention, the syncopated internal rhyme, the multi-layered allusions and popular culture motifs of today's Spoken Word artists reveal the influence of earlier writers and performers such as Haki Madhubuti, Gil Scott-Heron, Oscar Brown, Jr. and Nikki Giovanni. It has roots in Chicago's OBAC workshop and the writings of a poet such as Houston's Jarbari Aziz Ra — who was also an OBAC poet — show the elements of the Spoken Word style already *in print* in the late 1970s.

With Spoken Word, what we are looking at — or, perhaps better, listening to — may be the full development of a new poetic genre, an addition to both the oral and literary traditions. Of course the appearance of such poetry on the radio in the form of commercials for McDonald's or Oil of Olay cosmetics raises some other issues — the same issues of cultural allegiance, I suppose, raised by Ziggy Marley's reggae television spot for Cover Girl cosmetics.

The question of the intentions of our poets is, of course, a more complex matter than can be discussed here. If Larry Neal, Askia M. Touré, and Kalamu ya Salaam are correct to say that music — and by extension, poetry — is the most accurate index of the people's reality, what are we to make of the recent direction of "the changing same?"

Recent television documentaries recalling the March on Washington in 1963 raise a troubling question. What does it mean that in 40 years we have gone from singing "Woke up this mornin' with my mind stayed on freedom" to

Don't push me
Cause I'm close to the edge
I'm trying
Not to lose my head
Uh huh
It's a jungle out there
Sometimes it makes me wonder
How I keep from going under

to "Act a fool! Act a fool!"

We might merely conclude that the drum machine neither laughs nor weeps. It just keeps you dancing.

In a sense, then — mainly for extra-literary reasons, perhaps — the question of diversity in African American poetry can still be posited as a question of the relationship of African American people to the so-called "mainstream." Back in the awful days of the late 1960s, James Baldwin questioned the wisdom of what was then called "racial integration."

"Do we really want," he asked, "to be integrated into a burning house?"

Today, in our new colorblind society with African American music and comedy entertaining the entire planet, the question is — are such questions still even relevant?

On the other hand, as Alain Locke might have asked, what are African Americans if not Americans? When we follow Michael Jackson's instructions, who will we see in the mirror?

Robert E. May's recent book *Manifest Destiny's Underworld: Filibustering in Antebellum America* (2002) refers to the meaning of that word before it was applied to harangues in the United States Senate. May recounts attempts in the 1850s by American adventurers who tried to replicate the success of the Texas revolution by overthrowing South American countries in order to have them annexed as slave states. A reviewer of the book noted that, even though the world has changed since 9/11, "the story of the filibusters should humble Americans with the reminder that conspiracies to launch unprovoked attacks against neighboring states are not entirely foreign to us" (Miller 29).

Dare I say that an index of how far we have come will not only be found in our music or our poetry but might also be registered in the fact that the American government's current foreign policy principle of "preemptive warfare" is a philosophy articulated by National Security Advisor Dr. Condoleezza Rice? That, perhaps, is an *Ebony* magazine "first" that we might not want to put on the Black History Month quiz.

It is a fact, too, that indicates to me — more than anything else — the absolute necessity for poetry that is written out of a sense that it is our *obligation* to accept this world as the world we have been given but our *duty* to make it better.

Now that I think about it, dancing may not be so bad after all. As a wise man once said, "We have got to dance our way out of this constriction."

We, the poets, have the task of finding the words to go with the music.

WORKS CITED

Brown, Sterling A. "Slim Greer." 1932. *The Last Ride of Wild Bill.* Detroit: Broadside Press, 1975. 23-25.

Cullen, Countee, ed. *Caroling Dusk: An Anthology of verse by Negro poets.* New York: Harper, 1927.

---. "Pagan Prayer." 1925. *My Soul's High Song: The Collected Writings of Countee Cullen, Voice of the Harlem Renaissance.* Ed. Gerald Early. New York: Anchor Books, 1991. 91-92.

Francis, Consuela. "(Re)Making a Difference: The Harlem Renaissance and the Anxiety of 1926." *Langston Hughes Review* 17 (Fall/Spring 2002): 49-59.

Frost, Elisabeth A. *The Feminist Avant-Garde in American Poetry.* Iowa City: University of Iowa Press, 2003.

Golding, Alan. *From Outlaw to Classic: Canons in American Poetry.* Madison: University of Wisconsin Press, 1995.

Grandmaster Flash and the Furious Five. "The Message." *The Roots of Rap CD.* 1996.

Jennings, Regina. "Poetry of the Black Panther Party: Metaphors of Militancy." *Journal of Black Studies* 29 (September 1998): 106-129.

Miller, Daniel R. "American Jihad." Rev. of *Manifest Destiny's Underworld: Filibustering in Antebellum America.* By Robert E. May. Books and Culture 9 (January/February 2003): 29.

Redding, J. Saunders. *To Make a Poet Black.* 1939. College Park, Maryland: McGrath Publishing, 1968.

Smith, Robert A. "The Poetry of Countee Cullen." *Phylon* 11 (1950): 216-221.

Thomas, Lorenzo. *Extraordinary Measures: Afrocentric Modernism and Twentieth-Century American Poetry.* Tuscaloosa and London: University of Alabama Press, 2000.

Walton, Eda Lou. "On the Trail of Negro Song." *Poetry: A Magazine of Verse* 27 (January 1926): 221-226.

Contributors

Photograph by Lynda Koolish

JEFFERY RENARD ALLEN

Born in Chicago in 1962, Jeffery Renard Allen is currently an Associate Professor of English at Queens College of The City University of New York and an instructor in the MFA writing program at New School University. He has published two books, *Harbors and Spirits*, a collection of poems, and the novel, *Rails Under My Back*, which won *The Chicago Tribune*'s Heartland Prize for Fiction. Other awards include a Whiting Writer's Award and an honor for Pioneering Achievements in Fiction from the African American Literature and Culture Association. His essays, reviews, fiction, and poetry have appeared in numerous publications and anthologies, including *Poets & Writers, Ploughshares, Bomb, The Antioch Review, Hambone, StoryQuarterly, Callaloo, Other Voices, Notre Dame Review, Review, XCP: Cross Cultural Poetics, 110 Stories: New York Writes after September 11*, and *Step into the World: A Global Anthology of Black Literature*. Forthcoming books include *Stellar Places*, a second collection of poems, and *Bread and the Land*, a book of stories. Allen is also at work on a new novel, *Song of the Shank*, a narrative based on the life of the brilliant and controversial nineteenth-century pianist and composer Blind Tom.

Photograph by Lynda Koolish

HERMAN BEAVERS

Herman Beavers is an Associate Professor of English at the University of Pennsylvania, where he also serves as Acting Director of the Center for Africana Studies during the 2004–05 academic year. He received his BA in Government, Sociology, and Creative Writing from Oberlin College (1981). He went on to the Graduate Writing Program at Brown, where he received the MA in Creative Writing (1983). In 1985, he received an

MA from the Afro-American Studies Program at Yale Univeristy and in 1990 completed his doctorate in American Studies, also at Yale. He has been at the University of Pennsylvania since 1989. Since arriving there, he has authored the book *Wrestling Angels into Song: The Fictions of Ernest J. Gaines and James Alan McPherson* (U of Penn Press, 1995), as well as over 25 articles and book chapters. He has guest-edited issues of both *African American Review* and *Narrative* and he has either served or is serving on the editorial boards of *American Literature, Modern Fiction Studies, Modern Literary Studies,* and *African American Review.* His creative works include the chapbook *A Neighborhood of Feeling* as well as poems that have appeared in *Rain, Black American Literature Forum* (now *African American Review*), *Dark Phrases, The Cincinnati Poetry Review, Cave Canem I* and *II, Callaloo* and most recently, *Xconnect.*

Photograph by Lynda Koolish

WANDA COLEMAN

Wanda Coleman's fiction currently appears in *Crab Orchard Review, Fiction International, High Plains Literary Review, Obsidian III, Other Voices* and *Zyzzyva*. New poems appear in *88: A Journal, Poetry International* and *River Styx*. She is a former columnist for the *Los Angeles Times Magazine*. Her recent books from Black Sparrow Press are *Bathwater Wine*, winner of the 1999 Lenore Marshall Poetry Prize, *Mambo Hips & Make Believe* (a novel), and *Mercurochrome: New Poems*, bronze-medal finalist in the National Book Awards 2001. She received a California Arts Council fellowship in poetry in 2002. She is C.O.L.A.'s first literary fellow, Dept. of Cultural Affairs, Los Angeles, 2003-04 in fiction. Her new books are *Ostinato Vamps,* Pitt Poetry Series 2003-2004, and *Wanda Coleman's Greatest Hits: 1966-2003*, Pudding House Press, 2004. *The Riot Inside Me: More Trials & Temors* (autobiographical prose) is forthcoming (Godine, 2005).

Photograph by Lynda Koolish

C. S. GISCOMBE

C. S. Giscombe teaches in the MFA program at Penn State. His recent poetry books include *Here* and *Giscome Road. Into and Out of Dislocation* is a collection of Giscombe's essays. Works in progress include a poetry book about the midwest, *Prairie Style*, and a prose book about trains and train metaphors, titled *Traveling Public.*

Photograph by Lynda Koolish

ERIC GOODMAN

Eric Goodman, who directed the Marjorie Cook Conference on Diversity in African American Poetry, teaches in and directs the Creative Writing program at Miami University. He has published four novels: *Child of My Right Hand* (Sourcebooks, 2004); *In Days of Awe* (Alfred A.Knopf, 1991); *The First Time I Saw Jenny Hall* (William Morrow, 1983); and *High on the Energy Bridge* (Holt, Rinehart & Winston, 1980). Other publications include a handful of short stories and non-fiction pieces in national publications including *Saveur, GQ, Travel & Leisure, Los Angeles Times Sunday Magazine, Buzz, Glamour, Life,* and *Self.*

Photograph by Lynda Koolish

TERRANCE HAYES

Terrance Hayes is the author of *Hip Logic* (Penguin, 2002) and *Muscular Music* (Tia Chucha Press, 1999) and has been a recipient of many awards and prizes including a Whiting Writers Award, the Kate Tufts Discovery Award, a National Poetry Series award, a Pushcart Prize, a Best American Poetry selection, and a National Endowment for the Arts Fellowship. *Wind in a Box*, his third book, is forthcoming from Penguin in the spring of 2006. A South Carolina native, Hayes lives in Pittsburgh,

Pennsylvania with his family and is an Associate Professor of Creative Writing at Carnegie Mellon University.

Photograph by Lynda Koolish

KIM HUNTER

Kim Derrick Hunter was born in Detroit to African American working class parents in 1955. He has been a factory worker, a security guard, a middle school teacher and a street outreach worker. But most of his adult life has been spent working in media, primarily television and radio. The major influences on his work have been Cummings, Baraka, surrealist film and the post-industrial Detroit poetry scene. His work has appeared in a variety of journals including: *Triage, Hipology, The Metro Times, Dispatch, Graffiti Rag* and *+R (Plus D'art).* Past Tents Press published Hunter's first collection of poems, *borne on slow knives*, in 2001.

Photograph by Lynda Koolish

HONORÉE FANONNE JEFFERS

Both a poet and a fiction writer, Honorée Fanonne Jeffers has published two books of poetry, *The Gospel of Barbecue* and *Outlandish Blues*. She has won an award from the Rona Jaffe Foundation, and poetry fellowships from the MacDowell Colony and the Bread Loaf Writers Conference. Her work has appeared in *American Poetry Review*, *Brilliant Corners*, *Callaloo*, *Indiana Review*, *Iowa Review*, *The Kenyon Review*, and *New England Review*. A native Southerner, Honorée now lives in Oklahoma where she teaches at the University of Oklahoma and is at work on her first novel.

Photograph by Janette Kiehn

LYNDA KOOLISH

The work of photographer Lynda Koolish is in the permanent collections of the Schomburg Center for Research in Black Culture, the Hormel Center of the San Francisco Public Library, the San Diego State University Library, the Berg Collection of the New York Public Library, and the University of California Department of African American Studies. Her photographs have been widely exhibited, including one-woman shows at the Schomburg, the Jewett Gallery of the San Francisco Public Library, the San Diego State University Library, the University of California Townsend Center for the Humanities, the Salt Lake City Public Library, the Modern Language Association, the American Literature Association, and the Rosenberg Gallery at Goucher College. She also been in group shows at Lincoln Center for the Performing Arts in New York City, and at 871 Fine Arts Gallery in San Francisco. Currently a Professor of English and Comparative Literature at San Diego State University, she is the author and photographer of *African American Writers: Portraits and Visions*, a University Press of Mississippi collection of photographic portraits and literary biographies.

Photograph by Lynda Koolish

NATHANIEL MACKEY

Born in Miami, Florida in 1947, Nathaniel Mackey grew up, from age four, in California. He is the author of five chapbooks of poetry, *Four for Trane* (Golemics, 1978), *Septet for the End of Time* (Boneset, 1983), *Outlantish* (Chax Press, 1992), *Song of the Andoumboulou: 18-20* (Moving Parts Press, 1994) and *Four for Glenn* (Chax Press, 2002), and three books of poetry, *Eroding Witness* (University of Illinois Press, 1985), *School of Udhra* (City Lights Books, 1993) and *Whatsaid Serif* (City Lights Books, 1998). *Strick: Song of the Andoumboulou 16-25*, a compact disc recording of poems read with musical accompaniment (Royal Hartigan, percussion; Hafez Modirzadeh, reeds and flutes), was released in 1995 by Spoken Engine Company. He is also the author of an ongoing prose composition, *From a Broken Bottle Traces of Perfume Still Emanate*, of which three volumes have been published: *Bedouin Hornbook* (Callaloo Fiction Series, 1986; second edition: Sun & Moon Press, 1997), *Djbot Baghostus's Run* (Sun & Moon Press, 1993) and *Atet A.D.* (City Lights Books, 2001). He is editor of the literary magazine *Hambone* and co-editor (with Art Lange) of the anthology *Moment's Notice: Jazz in Poetry and Prose* (Coffee House Press, 1993). He is the author of two books of criticism, *Discrepant Engagement: Dissonance, Cross-Culturality, and Experimental Writing* (Cambridge University Press, 1993; paper edition: University of Alabama Press, 2000) and *Paracritical Hinge: Essays, Talks, Notes, Interviews* (University of Wisconsin Press, 2005). His awards and honors include the selection of *Eroding Witness* for publication in the National Poetry Series, a Whiting Writer's Award in 1993 and election to the Board of Chancellors of the Academy of American Poets in 2001. He is Professor of Literature at the University of California, Santa Cruz.

Photograph by Lynda Koolish

TRACIE MORRIS

Tracie Morris is a poet who has worked in a variety of genres including print, multimedia installation, recorded work, visual media and live performance. She holds multiple degrees from Hunter College, CUNY and New York University. Morris has taught at Queens College, CUNY, SUNY Purchase and Sarah Lawrence College.

Photograph by Lynda Koolish

HARRYETTE MULLEN

Harryette Mullen's poems, short stories, and essays have been published widely and reprinted in over 40 anthologies. Her poetry is included in the latest edition of the *Norton Anthology of African American Literature* and has been translated into Spanish, French, Polish, and Bulgarian. She is the author of six poetry books, most recently *Blues Baby* (Bucknell, 2002) and *Sleeping with the Dictionary* (University of California, 2002). The latter was a finalist for a National Book Award, National Book Critics Circle Award, and Los Angeles Times Book Prize. In 2004 she received an award from the Foundation for Contemporary Performance Arts. She was born in Alabama, grew up in Texas, and now lives in Los Angeles, where she teaches at UCLA.

Photograph by Lynda Koolish

ALDON NIELSEN

Aldon Lynn Nielsen is the Kelly Professor of American Literature at Pennsylvania State University. His books of criticism include *Integral Music: Languages of African American Innovation, Black Chant: Languages of African American Postmodernism, Writing Between the Lines, C.L.R. James: A Critical Introduction* and *Reading Race*. He was the first winner of the Larry Neal Award for poetry, and his volumes of poetry include *Mixage, Vext, Heat Strings, Evacuation Routes* and *Stepping Razor*. The anthology *Every Goodbye Ain't Gone*, which he co-edited with Lauri Ramey, is forthcoming from the University of Alabama Press.

Photograph by Lynda Koolish

MENDI LEWIS OBADIKE

Mendi Lewis Obadike is the author of *Armor and Flesh: Poems* and the libretto for an internet opera entitled *The Sour Thunder*. Her text-based new media art has been commissioned by the Whitney Museum of American Art, Yale University, and the New York African Film Festival and Electronic Arts Intermix, among other institutions. She received a Rockefeller New Media Award to develop *TaRonda, Who Wore White Gloves,* an opera which explores black codes of conduct. She will develop *Four Electric Ghosts* (an opera based on Amos Tutuola's novel *My Life in the Bush of Ghosts* and the video game Pac Man) in Toni Morrison's Atelier at Princeton in the fall of 2005. Mendi lives and works with her husband Keith in the New York metropolitan area.

Photograph by Lynda Koolish

JAMES RICHARDSON

James W. Richardson lives, creates, and teaches in Atlanta, Georgia, where he is completing his dissertation, "Theorizing a Diasporic Aesthetic in African American and Jewish American 20th-Century Autobiography."

Photograph by Lynda Koolish

TIM SEIBLES

Tim Seibles is the author of *Hammerlock, Body Moves* and *Hurdy-Gurdy*. His newest collection, *Buffalo Head Solos*, has just been released by the Cleveland State University Poetry Center. He is a former NEA fellow and received an Open Voice Award from the 63rd Street Y in New York City. His work has been featured in anthologies such as *Humor Me, Role Call, Outsiders*, and *The Poets' Grimm*. He has led workshops for Cave Canem — a retreat for black writers — and for the Zora Neale Hurston/Richard Wright Foundation. He lives in Norfolk, Virginia, where he is a member of Old Dominion University's English Department and MFA in Writing faculty.

Photograph by Catherine Hennessy

KATHY LOU SCHULTZ

Kathy Lou Schultz's collections of poetry and experimental fiction are *Some Vague Wife* (Atelos Press), *Genealogy* (a+bend press), and *Re dress* (San Francisco State University) – winner of the Michael Rubin Award. Her work has recently been published in *Fence, Hambone*, and *Biting the Error: Writers Explore Narrative* (Coach House Press). She received her MFA from San Francisco State University and is currently an advanced PhD student in English at the University of Pennsylvania where her research focuses on Afro-Modernist poetry. She is a co-founder of the journal *Lipstick Eleven.*

Photograph by Lynda Koolish

REGINALD SHEPHERD

Reginald Shepherd is the editor of *The Iowa Anthology of New American Poetries*, published by the University of Iowa Press in 2004. His fourth book of poems, *Otherhood*, was published by the University of Pittsburgh Press in 2003; it was a finalist for the 2004 Lenore Marshall Poetry Prize and for a 2004 Lambda Literary Award. His other books, all published by Pittsburgh, are *Some Are Drowning*, winner of the 1993 Associated Writing Programs' Award in Poetry; *Angel, Interrupted*, a finalist for a 1997 Lambda Literary Award; and *Wrong*. Winner of a 1993 "Discovery"/*The Nation* Award, Shepherd has received grants from the NEA, the Illinois Arts Council, the Constance Saltonstall Foundation, and the Ludwig Vogelstein Foundation, among other awards and honors; his work has also appeared in four editions of *The Best American Poetry*. He currently lives and writes in Pensacola, Florida.

Photograph by Lynda Koolish

EVIE SHOCKLEY

Evie Shockley is the author of *The Gorgon Goddess* (Carolina Wren Press, 2001). Her poetry also appears in print and online in *African American Review, Beloit Poetry Journal, Brilliant Corners, Bum Rush the Page: A Def Poetry Jam, Callaloo, Crab Orchard Review, Hambone, HOW2, nocturnes (re)view of the literary arts, Poetry Daily: Poems from the World's Most Popular Poetry Website,* and other journals and anthologies. She was awarded a residency at the Hedgebrook Retreat for Women Writers in 2003 and belongs to several poetry communities, including Cave Canem, the Lucifer Poetics Group, and the Carolina African American Writers Collective. Shockley, who earned her PhD at Duke University in 2002, is Assistant Professor of English at Wake Forest University. Her current academic projects include a book tentatively titled *Gothic Homelessness: Domestic Ideology, Identity, and Social Terror in African American Literature* and an investigation of the relationship of race and innovation in African American poetry.

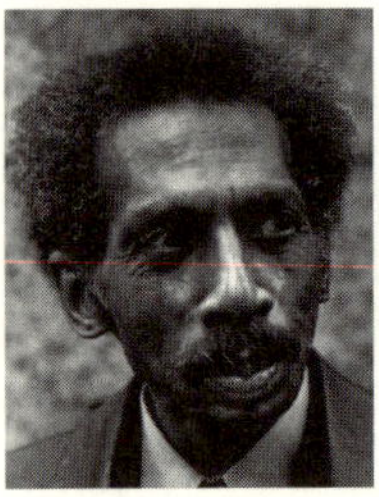

Photograph by Lynda Koolish

LORENZO THOMAS (1944-2005)

Lorenzo Thomas, one of the leading poets and critics of his generation, died on July 4th, 2005 as this book was in production. His reading and plenary address were among the highlights of the conference, and in recognition of his role as friend and guiding spirit to many poets and scholars at the conference, this anthology is dedicated to his memory. Lorenzo Thomas is the author of *Extraordinary Measures: Afrocentric Modernism and 20th-Century American Poetry* (named a 2001 Choice Outstanding Academic Book) and several collections of poetry including *Dancing on Main Street, Chances Are Few,* and *The Bathers.* He also edited *Sing the Sun Up: Creative Writing Ideas from African American Literature.* Thomas was Professor of English at University of Houston-Downtown.

Photograph by Lynda Koolish

NATASHA TRETHEWEY

Natasha Trethewey is the author of *Bellocq's Ophelia* (Graywolf, 2002) and *Domestic Work* (Graywolf, 2000). Her third collection, *Native Guard*, is forthcoming from Houghton Mifflin. She is the recipient of fellowships from the Guggenheim Foundation, the Rockefeller Foundation Bellagio Study Center, the NEA, and the Bunting Fellowship Program of the Radcliffe Institute for Advanced Study at Harvard. Her poems have appeared in such journals and anthologies as *American Poetry Review, Callaloo, Kenyon Review, The Southern Review, New England Review, Gettysburg Review*, and *The Best American Poetry* 2000 and 2003. Currently, she is Associate Professor of English and Creative Writing at Emory University. During the 2005–2006 academic year, she will hold the Lehman-Brady Joint Chair Professorship of Documentary and American Studies at Duke and UNC Chapel Hill.

Photograph by Lynda Koolish

KEITH TUMA

Keith Tuma is the author of *Fishing by Obstinate Isles: Modern and Postmodern British Poetry and American Readers* (Northwestern, 1998). He is the editor of *Anthology of Twentieth-Century British and Irish Poetry* (Oxford, 2001) and co-editor of *Mina Loy: Woman and Poet* (NPF, 1998) and *Additional Apparitions: Poetry, Performance & Site-Specifity* (The Cherry-on-Top Press, 2002). His essays on British, Irish, American, and Anglophone poetry have appeared in many journals and in a number of books edited by others, including *Assembling Alternatives: Reading Postmodern Poetries Transnationally* and *The Cambridge History of Twentieth-Century English Literature*. His poems and performance texts have appeared in journals including *Chicago Review, Notre Dame Review, Open Letter, Poetry Salzburg, The Gig, nth position, Flights, Famous Reporter*, and in the anthologies *100 Days* and *Onsets*. His chapbook of poetic squibs and epigrams *Topical Ointment* was published by Slack Buddha Press in 2004. *Critical Path: Into the Bush*, the first volume of an ongoing collaboration with cris cheek and William R. Howe, appeared in 2003. He is currently Acting Editor of Miami University Press and Professor and Chair of the English Department at Miami University.

Photograph by Lynda Koolish

ANTHONY WALTON

Anthony Walton is the author of *Mississippi: An American Journey*. He teaches at Bowdoin College in Brunswick, Maine.

Photograph by Lynda Koolish

CRYSTAL WILLIAMS

Crystal Williams, a native of Detroit, Michigan, is the author of *Kin* and *Lunatic*. Her work appears in many journals and anthologies, including *5AM, Callaloo, Ms. Magazine, Indiana Review, Court Green, American Poetry: The Next Generation, Poetry Nation,* and *Beyond the Frontier*. She holds degrees from NYU and Cornell University.

Photograph by Owen Carey

TYRONE WILLIAMS

Tyrone Williams teaches literature and literary theory at Xavier University in Cincinnati, Ohio. Recent publications include two chapbooks, *AAB* (Slack Buddha Press, 2004) and *Futures, Elections* (Dos Madres Press, 2004).

Acknowledgements

Jeffery Renard Allen
"Prayer to Eshbu-Elegba" was published in *The Literary Review*. "Mud Wit" is scheduled to appear in *Arkansas Review*.

Wanda Coleman
"The African Beneath the American" is from *Ostinato Vamps: Poems*, by Wanda Coleman, © 2003. Reprinted by permission of the University of Pittsburgh Press.

C. S. Giscombe
"Light, Bright, Etc." first appeared in *The Gig*. "Negromania, Negrophilia, Negrophobia" first appeared in *Court Green*.

Honorée Fanonne Jeffers
"Philly in the Light" first appeared in *Callaloo*, but has since appeared in Jeffers' book of poetry, *The Gospel of Barbecue*, along with "Tuscaloosa: Riversong."

Nathaniel Mackey
"Song of the Andoumboulou: 58" was published in *Enough*, ed. Rick London and Leslie Scalapino (Oakland: O Books, 2003). "Song of the Andoumboulou: 62" appeared first in *The Gig*, 16 (February 2004). "Song of the Andoumboulou: 58" is forthcoming in *Splay Anthem* (New Directions, Spring 2006).

Harryette Mullen
"El Malecón," "Poetry for Dummies," "Summer Salt," and "Drinking Mojitos in Cuba Libre" all appeared in *Callaloo*, ed. Charles Rowell. "Drinking Mojitos in Cuba Libre" also appeared in *X-tra*, ed. Allan deSouza, and *Volt*, eds. Calvin Bedient and Gillian Conoley. "#6 Sepulveda" and "Broken Glish" also appeared previously in *Volt*.

"Mermaid of Palmares" first appeared in *Hambone*, ed. Nathaniel Mackey. "Headlines," "Unacknowledged Legislator," and "Bumper to Bumper" have appeared previously in *Open City*, ed. Lee Ann Brown.

Mendi Lewis Obadike
"Fifteen" and "Protest Poem" were first published in Obadike's *Armor and Flesh: Poems*, from Lotus Press.

Tim Seibles
"Douglass, A Last Letter" will be published by the journal *Third Coast* in the fall of 2005.

Lorenzo Thomas
"Downtown Boom" appeared in the anthology *Texas in Poetry 2* edited by Billy Bob Hill (Fort Worth: Texas Christian University Press, 2002). Reprinted by permission of the author. "Discovering America Again," and "Souvenir of the Manassah Ball" © 1979, 2003 by Lorenzo Thomas. Reprinted here from *Chances Are Few* by permission of Blue Wind Press.

Natasha Trethewey
"Bellocq's Ophelia," "Letter Home," "(Self) Portrait," and "Vignette" © 2002 by Nathasha Trethewey. Reprinted from *Bellocq's Ophelia* by permission of Graywolf Press, Saint Paul, Minnesota.

Anthony Walton
All poems © Anthony Walton. "Gwendolyn Brooks" and "The Encyclopedia of Rhythm and Blues" first appeared in *The New Yorker*. "Dissidence" first appeared in *River Styx*.

Crystal Williams
"Ritual" and "On Forgetting" are both to appear in *Court Green*. "Negro Survival..." appeared previously in the *Indiana Review*.